Payday Lending

Other Palgrave Pivot titles

Lisa Lau and Om Prakash Dwivedi: **Re-Orientalism and Indian Writing in English**

Chapman Rackaway: **Communicating Politics Online**

G. Douglas Atkins: **T.S. Eliot's Christmas Poems: An Essay in Writing-as-Reading and Other "Impossible Unions"**

Marsha Berry and Mark Schleser: **Mobile Media Making in an Age of Smartphones**

Isabel Harbaugh: **Smallholders and the Non-Farm Transition in Latin America**

Daniel A. Wagner: **Learning and Education in Developing Countries: Research and Policy for the Post-2015 UN Development Goals**

Murat Ustaoğlu and Ahmet İncekara: **Islamic Finance Alternatives for Emerging Economies: Empirical Evidence from Turkey**

Laurent Bibard: **Sexuality and Globalization: An Introduction to a Phenomenology of Sexualities**

Thorsten Botz-Bornstein and Noreen Abdullah-Khan: **The Veil in Kuwait: Gender, Fashion, Identity**

Vasilis Kostakis and Michel Bauwens: **Network Society and Future Scenarios for a Collaborative Economy**

Tom Watson (editor): **Eastern European Perspectives on the Development of Public Relations: Other Voices**

Erik Paul: **Australia as US Client State: The Geopolitics of De-Democratization and Insecurity**

Floyd Weatherspoon: **African-American Males and the U.S. Justice System of Marginalization: A National Tragedy**

Mark Axelrod: **No Symbols Where None Intended: Literary Essays from Laclos to Beckett**

Paul M. W. Hackett: **Facet Theory and the Mapping Sentence: Evolving Philosophy, Use and Application**

Irwin Wall: **France Votes: The Election of François Hollande**

David J. Staley: **Brain, Mind and Internet: A Deep History and Future**

Georgiy Voloshin: **The European Union's Normative Power in Central Asia: Promoting Values and Defending Interests**

Shane McCorristine: **William Corder and the Red Barn Murder: Journeys of the Criminal Body**

Catherine Blair: **Securing Pension Provision: The Challenge of Reforming the Age of Entitlement**

Zarlasht M. Razeq: **UNDP's Engagement with the Private Sector, 1994–2011**

James Martin: **Drugs on the Dark Net: How Cryptomarkets Are Transforming the Global Trade in Illicit Drugs**

Shin Yamashiro: **American Sea Literature: Seascapes, Beach Narratives, and Underwater Explorations**

Sudershan Goel, Barbara A. Sims, and Ravi Sodhi: **Domestic Violence Laws in the United States and India: A Systematic Comparison of Backgrounds and Implications**

Gregory Sandstrom: **Human Extension: An Alternative to Evolutionism, Creationism and Intelligent Design**

palgrave▶pivot

Payday Lending: Global Growth of the High-Cost Credit Market

Carl Packman
Independent Researcher, London, UK

DOI: 10.1057/9781137361103.0001

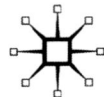

PAYDAY LENDING
Copyright © Carl Packman, 2014.
All rights reserved.
First published in 2014 by
PALGRAVE MACMILLAN®
in the United States—a division of St. Martin's Press LLC,
175 Fifth Avenue, New York, NY 10010.

Where this book is distributed in the UK, Europe and the rest of the world, this is by Palgrave Macmillan, a division of Macmillan Publishers Limited, registered in England, company number 785998, of Houndmills, Basingstoke, Hampshire RG21 6XS.

Palgrave Macmillan is the global academic imprint of the above companies and has companies and representatives throughout the world.

Palgrave® and Macmillan® are registered trademarks in the United States, the United Kingdom, Europe and other countries.

ISBN: 978-1-137-36122-6 EPUB
ISBN: 978-1-137-36110-3 PDF
ISBN: 978-1-137-37280-2 Hardback

Library of Congress Cataloging-in-Publication Data is available from the Library of Congress.

A catalogue record of the book is available from the British Library.

First edition: 2014

www.palgrave.com/pivot

DOI: 10.1057/9781137361103

For Katherine O'Brien

Contents

Acknowledgments		vii
Introduction		1
1	The History and Development of High-Cost Credit and Payday Lending	4
2	Payday in the UK	36
3	The European Directive to Consume	55
4	The Australian SACCs Appeal	73
5	Back in North America	98
6	Discussion Points	114
7	Conclusion and Recommendations	133
Index		140

Acknowledgments

I am especially grateful to Jialan Wang at the Consumer Finance Protection Bureau, Stan Keyes at the Canadian Payday Loan Association, Nathan Groff at Veritec Solutions, Phil Johns at the National Financial Services Federation, Gerard Brody at the Consumer Action Law Group, Jodi Gardner at the University of Oxford, Johnna Montgomerie at Goldsmiths University, Professor Paul Ali at the Melbourne Law School, and the many others who I've spoken to over the years and who have shaped my thinking on the issue of high-cost credit. I would also like to thank my publisher Palgrave Macmillan for allowing me to write this volume.

palgrave▸pivot

www.palgrave.com/pivot

Introduction

Packman, Carl. *Payday Lending: Global Growth of the High-Cost Credit Market*. New York: Palgrave MacMillan, 2014. DOI: 10.1057/9781137361103.0003.

▶

With the matter of high-cost credit, particularly in the form of its most notorious and well-known variant payday lending, consumers have presented to them one of two conflicting assessments: on the one hand we have the numerous studies that have been critical of the industry in recent years, or we can believe the industry itself. I've been fortunate to bear witness to both. In 1999 UK "extortionate credit," of which payday lending was considered a growing yet significant part, had the following factors associated with it: high cost; dubious sales practices; lacking in transparency; odious means of debt recovery.[1] The industry on the other hand suggested otherwise. The Community Financial Services Association of America (CFSA), an association representing over half of the payday loan stores in the United States, has claimed that "payday advance customers represent the heart of America's middle class."[2]

Indeed if that industry representation doesn't suit, then maybe the following from Dan Feehan, the CEO of Cash America, in 2007 will: "[T]he theory in the business is [that] you've got to get that customer in, work to turn him into a repetitive customer, long-term customer, because that's really where the profitability is."[3]

What I have tried to do in this volume is test both hypotheses with the available evidence. I have done this by tracing the vast amounts of research in order to identify international commonalities and assess whether or not there *is* a global theme to payday lending and other forms of high-cost credit.

My wider assertion is that those countries that have seen a ballooning of payday lending in the recent years had not seen it coming. While debt has been an issue of concern for policymakers of countries the world over my suggestion is that the formalized high-cost credit industry—which to my definition are those consumer creditors that have taken liberally from salary lending, pawnbroking, and cash checking and developed a business primarily targeted at the working poor that has become normalized, globalized, while formally staying outside of the mainstream—slipped through the net almost unnoticed. There are some variations in this process. In some countries the practice was illegal until laws were changed to accommodate for it, while in other countries it existed for a good deal of time with little regulatory awareness. Similarly, now that the industry has become subject to what I call "heightened consciousness," owing to its controversial practices and eye-watering interest rates, many governments have in recent times been caught so unaware that they are now struggling to contain the growing problem of debt-distress within.

In all, what I have attempted to show is that the commonalities of what defines the industry, and the type of customer they tend to target and make money from, are so strong that there is a justified case for governments to take uniform action. My warning for consumers and policymakers of those countries, as well as others who might imagine theirs is far less likely a target, is that ignorance of the small gains of predatory loans companies could have, and indeed has, left countries on the back foot trying to temper a very different personal debt crisis to any that has previously been seen.

In Chapter 1, I assess the development of the formalized payday lending industry by placing it into the historical context of debt, consumerism, and the primacy of the individual over the welfare of communities. In Chapter 2, I begin to document the industry as it develops into one with international reach, firstly in the United Kingdom. In Chapter 3, I look at the industry's rather more difficult entrance into the wider European community. Chapter 4 picks up closely on the regulatory architecture of Australia, Chapter 5 returns to North America to see how it has progressed in its homeland, and in Chapters 6 and 7 I finish with a discussion of the findings and some conclusions and recommendations.

Notes

1 Kempson, E. and Whlyey, C. (1999), *Extortionate Credit in the UK*, London: Department of Trade and Industry.
2 Cited in Martin, Nathalie (2012), High-Interest Loans and Class: Do Payday and Title Loans Really Serve the Middle Class, *Loyola Consumer Law Review*, 524.
3 Quoted in Bocian, Davis, Garrison, Sermons (2012), *The State of Lending in America & Its Impact on U.S. Households*, US: Center for Responsible Lending.

1
The History and Development of High-Cost Credit and Payday Lending

Abstract: *Chapter 1 looks at the development of the formalized payday lending industry and its roots from salary lending to cash checking. It goes into detail about the part that positive perceptions of consumer credit had in the normalization of debt, before looking into the specific conditions that brought about high-cost credit more broadly.*

Keywords: cash checking; consumerism; credit; debt; loan sharks; payday lending

Packman, Carl. *Payday Lending: Global Growth of the High-Cost Credit Market.* New York: Palgrave MacMillan, 2014. DOI: 10.1057/9781137361103.0004.

Research shows that credit money has a long history dating all the way back to the beginning of civilization.¹ High-cost credit has existed for longer than money itself.² Even for the abridged story of high-cost credit as we know it today we have to go a long way back into the history of moneylending in the United States. Indeed as one study concludes, the practice of extending credit against a postdated check, such was the original means of carrying out a payday loan transaction, dates back at least to the Great Depression.³

Back then banks didn't extend credit to individuals as they do now; this practice was reserved largely for small businesses. To get credit before the 1920s one would have to visit a merchant or a country department store or hope to secure something from friends or family. If none of these were available then a pawnshop may extend a securitized loan, a philanthropic loan (such as from New York City's Provident Loan Society), commercial small loan lenders (like Household Finance), or a loan shark. According to the Community Reinvestment Association of North Carolina before the "consumer revolution" of the 1920s, poor and working-class Southerners relied on pawnbrokers, illegal small loan lenders, or family and friends; and, even from this early on the poorest in society paid the most for the finance they sought.

According to the Federal Census of 1920, there were 518 pawnbrokers and moneylenders in North Carolina alone⁴—however, we also know the extent to which reliable data on pawnbroking were to come by at this time. Indeed one study from the 1930s, that would question the rigor of the Federal Census, points out: "No national statistics of pawnbrokers have ever been compiled, nor, as far as the author has been able to find out, have any been published even for a single city."⁵ This is backed up by another study which concluded: "It is difficult to determine the exact number of pawnshops in the U.S., because there are entities that resemble pawnshops in some respects that should not be considered as pawnshops," that is to say that such firms were "often not licensed or regulated by the state and may operate only on weekends or travel from place to place."⁶

Only in the mid-1920s did commercial banks begin to make small loans, though at first only to wealthier customers. This may not have mattered too much to many low-income people. It has been noted that the ability to secure credit from friends or families, or even stores in the local area, would not have been as difficult as it sounds today in the modern world. One very interesting point made by Bruce G Curruthers and Laura Ariovich in their volume *Money and Credit: A Sociological Approach* was that before railroads most people traded locally and so local exchange "embedded people in their own personal social networks, and entailed obligations of neighborliness and civility."[7] As such debt, particularly in the late eighteenth and nineteenth centuries, was treated with forbearance, was more informal and flexible, and was loose on legal rectitude. Increasingly, however, in the nineteenth- century exchange became more long-distance as with transportation, and the trust that was maintained originally, in a more local setting, and with people who a debtor probably knew fairly well in the community, became rather strained as finance evolved into a transaction made between relative strangers.

One extremely important development occurred with the advent of installment lending, hire purchase being a popular variant in countries such as the UK, or informally as layaway, the "never-never" or lay-by in Australia and New Zealand. It is believed to be the successful experiment of Cyrus McCormack (1809–1884) and popularized by Issac Singer, the inventor and entrepreneur whose improvements to the sewing machine made it vitally easy for use in home settings before it became more common in 1930s America. Indeed this form of credit was associated with the purchase of relatively expensive household items such as sewing machines (Issac Singer knew what he was doing, clearly), furniture, tractors, pianos, and encyclopedia sets. Installment lending, however, had the greatest effect for the automobile industry. In 1900, around 1 percent of consumer spending was on automobiles. In 1910 that figure was 10.6 percent, and then 31.4 percent in 1925, when cars were on the mass market. By 1950 the typical urban family had spent around 12 percent of the annual income on installment payments alone.[8]

While banks were generally considered to be for the wealthy only, with everyone else catered for outside the conventional economy, installment lending provided those people who were formally outside the system to enjoy the fruits—for what they were worth—of capitalism and consumerism. However, this form of credit was not so altruistic. Let's suppose that the cash price of an item is $100, a customer would give $10 as a down payment, and agree to pay the additional finance of $100 over the following 10 months. At that point a finance company would buy an installment contract of $100 for $83. The retailer, therefore, would immediately have $93. For that $83 the finance company who bought the installment contract would get $100 over the next 10 months. In addition to that the finance company would pay a retailer a collection fee of 10 percent, meaning that upon completion, assuming all payments were made, the retailer would receive an additional $10. In total the retailer would end up in receipt of $103 from an installment sale rather than $100 from the cash sale. It has been worked out by Louis Hyman that the finance company over ten months would make $7 for a total investment of $90, equivalent to 21.7 percent. On this basis a company could expect to make $20,000 with $100,000 worth of accounts.[9]

The plight of African Americans trying to find access to finance in order to borrow for household items was even more complicated. While mainstream financiers wouldn't dare lend to a group of people with as much stigma attached, black Americans found themselves more often than not led into the hands of loan sharks and other predatory lenders. Indeed one only had to look in the pages of magazines and current affairs publications read primarily by blacks at the time. The pages of African American newspapers like the *Chicago Defender* and the *New York Amsterdam News* overloaded its readers with adverts about access to the "easiest credit terms" on "attractive bedroom and dining room sets."[10] Similarly installment loans salesmen, it would point out in their reports, went about reassuring borrowers that "if there were any problems meeting the payments...'leniency' would be shown." It is said, however, that if borrowers could pay off the furniture "the retailer would make money, but more profit actually would be had if they made a few payments and then defaulted."[11] It is a familiar story, even today, but profit maximization comes from trapping borrowers, in whatever form of borrowing there is.

Carrying over fees on installment loans, instead of paying back on time and in full, came with no profit incentive for the seller, and thus with no legal or regulatory oversight this type of lending found itself awash with predators. Indeed such regulatory oversight occurred later on where usury laws covered some small-dollar loans and loan sharks, but failed to cover installment lenders. Either regulators were unwise to the problem of predatory installment lending, or it was a calculated attempt to allow it to go unnoticed in order that mainstream finance didn't have to *do business* with a certain clientèle.

Indeed the Legal Aid Society reported that often no leniency was shown and, to top it off, while borrowers would be shown new items at the suite, what they would actually be sold was repossessed furniture that had been polished. For this pleasure, by the 1920s the percentage of loans used to consolidate other loans, mostly installment loans, stood at around 50–75 percent. Therefore, it was certainly not beyond the realms of possibility that a large number of people would struggle to pay back money on installment loans for purchases, fail to receive the purchases they requested, or receive knock-off equivalents that have had a lick of polish to cover up the cracks (literally). They might then find themselves in a situation where additional loans were needed, from various lenders, to consolidate those loans.

During 1899–1900, it was found that credit sales made to the T.C. Power and Bro. Department store made up around 78 percent of total sales. Indeed the rise of T.C. Power and Bro., particularly over 1870–1902, is an underappreciated benchmark from which many other small department stores based their commercialization strategies. One of the main strategies was issuing credit to its main customers. Low prices and product diversification were of utmost importance, while allowing substantial credit loans to farmers, including cattle and sheep farmers, was a way to keep customers coming back.

Historians have traditionally focused on larger stores for an insight into what inspired modern means of retail, and keeping a solid custom base, but T.C., a small, family run department store in Montana, with its incentives to nurture return custom based on trust and extending credit products, which would later inspire other more modern forms of credit, including store cards, is clearly the driving force for a service that is responsive to economic realities, social needs (we might think of large grocery stores and reward points cards), and the future of the consumer west.[12]

Bigger stores such as Sears, Roebuck & Company or Macy's aimed to buck this trend by dealing only in cash at lower prices. For them it was hoped that a customer's loyalty would follow the low cost. This was not to last. The trend was not bucked, which indicated to all retailers just where the revolution was headed. Credit, as it was said at the time, was just "too effective a tool for selling to consumers."[13]

With the rise of the consumer, retailers embracing consumer credit, whether out of principle or by having their hands tied by the zeitgeist, it became more necessary to check on the types of credit being sold, particularly irresponsible loans from predatory lenders. It was vitally necessary to do this as the growth in the consumer, on a wide scale, would still only benefit a more affluent household.

Consumer credit bureaus emerged in the late nineteenth century, but remained local. The largest of its kind in New York oversaw around

75,000 individuals. Philanthropic organizations like New York-based Russell Sage Foundation mobilized public opinion against loan sharks, the foremost predatory lender, after more attractive credit options began to dry up in the early twentieth century. The foundation made supporting remedial loan societies like the Provident Loan Society of New York, which offered below market rate loans to the poorest, its raison d'être. It took a huge deal of time to really take off. The concern of the early loan societies was that low-income consumers were not only being excluded from the spoils of a society that allowed middle class consumers to borrow and enjoy the consumerist revolution on future income, but that for even a glimpse of this new life the poor were having to spend a premium. On the one hand advertising agencies were selling a new life on the never–never for a classless consumer society, but the means of affording such a lifestyle were denied on the grounds of income. Put to one side the idea that one ought to save before buying items, the new credit-based economy would encourage the middle class to say: make your payday today.

As the Russell Sage Foundation focused its efforts on creating new laws on affordable credit, it was Edward Filene of the Twentieth Century Fund who became the chief proponent of credit unions. Filene was the businessman and philanthropist better known for building the Filene's department stores, shop locations of which were from 1986 converted into Macy's stores (seeing Macy's go full circle from being cash-only at the beginning of the twentieth century to merging with stores built by one of America's most pioneering advocates and practitioners of credit unions), and whose fund helped establish the Credit Union Extension Bureau in 1921. Legislation to enable credit unions had already passed first in Massachusetts in 1909, then in New York and Texas in 1913. Come 1915, some 64 credit unions had established, and by 1925 there were 284. From 1929 to 1939 the number of credit unions grew from 974 to 7,000. By the 1940s a similar version of the Uniform Small Loan Law existed in 34 states and many companies operated under its auspices. This also reflected the movement toward greater personal loans from mainstream banks, for which there were very few before the 1920s. What this period also reflected was not just types of credit, but debt profiles: non-mortgage consumer debt, as a proportion of household income, rose from 4.6 percent in 1919 to 11.4 percent in 1939.[14]

Owing to the growth of predatory lenders, particularly in places such as Chicago where they were far better documented and notorious, usury laws, tough rules on small-dollar loans, and interest rate ceilings were the norm in the United States. But there is nothing new about them. It might be assumed that early usury laws were the upshot of a particularly religious imperative against the moneylenders, though this is not necessarily the case. The first usury law was adopted by Massachusetts colony in 1641, predating the US constitution by nearly 150 years. It has been assumed that owing to the strong Christian overtones of the law books at the time that usury was an extension of this. As John Augustus Bolles has said on usury, "Amongst their earliest statute offenses we find enumerated idolatry, blasphemy, witchcraft, and cursing or smiting, one's father—all which were punished with death. We might, therefore, well expect to find among those laws a severe denunciation against usury."[15]

Indeed this seems like a fair assumption. But what must be said about the usury laws of the founding Fathers? While they disagreed on a great many things, on the question of an interest rate cap set at 8 percent there was little debate. Was the United States built on Christian foundations? The argument around this question is as old as the legacy of the Fathers themselves. But with quotes such as "Congress shall make NO law respecting an establishment of religion, or prohibiting the free exercise thereof; or abridging the freedom of speech, or of the press; or the right of the people peaceably to assemble, and to petition the government for a redress of grievances,"[16] clearly the question of Christian foundations is at most ambiguous, likely untrue. And while there is a Christian argument against usury it is inconclusive whether or not it is from a national Christian instinct that laws against usury have persevered in the United States.

Demonstrably unperturbed by the ongoing debates around the ethics of lending money with interest, it was during the 1930s that it was more widely realized by banks that a bit of money could be made by selling personal loans to those who were otherwise outside of the mainstream. Commercial banks for a period would extend "accommodation" loans to those who had already borrowed large sums of money for their businesses—meaning that this type of personal loan was already catered toward a certain consumer. It might also be argued, however, that this type of loan was a necessary correlative to keeping on customers, especially customers with businesses. The banks would not be able to make too much money on these loans but would deal in them anyway, perhaps in the hope that this was another way of keeping a customer on the books.[17]

National City was one of the first to offer personal loans in 1928, while the Hudson County National Bank followed that lead. Before taking out a loan with First Wisconsin Bank one had to have deposited at least $1. The rules attached to them, even perhaps by today's standards, seem rather strict. For example, it would "not entertain a personal loan under any circumstances to help buy a luxury or for speculative purposes." Louis Hyman points out that: "While we today might doubt the sincerity of their moralistic language, the strange repayment plans for these loans demonstrated that bankers put rehabilitating debtors' habits before profitability"[18]—quite a clear departure from many of the practices today, one might argue.

A typical charge on loans was around $8 on every $100 over the course of 12 months, which represented a 16 percent interest rate. A mid-Western banker by the name of Cornelius Clark in 1932 penned a letter in a banking trade magazine saying that a bank would only profit by around 11 cents, since the gross profit of the $8 would go directly on staff expenses, investigation, advertising, and then finally collection.[19] Given the direction of travel by the late 1930s the personal debt was no longer seen as "evil"; loan balances in many banks exceeded those of credit unions, equaled those of industrial banks, matched those of small loan companies who would still operate and cater to working class citizens.

The development of the American consumer

In postwar America, with limited interruptions and an economy on the mend, plans were circulating to develop the individual consumer. It has been presumed by Carruthers and Ariovich that this plan was an attempt to make capitalism look on the side of the normal man and woman on the street again, after a dip in economic confidence post-Depression. The consequences of this were that more than ever before Americans were able to go into deeper debt than ever before. As it was, after World War II American became a mass consumer society, one that Lizabeth Cohen would dub a "consumer republic."[20] With house buying, automobiles, durable goods, and other commodities, it was realized that American consumers were the driving force for economic growth, without the burden of having to plan an economy or develop measures toward a redistributional welfare state in the style of many postwar European countries, then despite the debt consequences it looked as though the magic bullet was in credit.

The underconsumptionist theories of the interwar period and the great depression won the battle of ideas; the contention was that the overwhelming economic problem of the day was insufficient demand, which in turn led to "under-consumption, low prices, low investment, and slow growth." In hindsight it was supposed that Americans were hard-working and reaped honest rewards rather than be taken with the falsehoods of consumer credit—that was until the hedonism of the 1950s led normal US citizens down a dishonest path. This overindividualist critique, however, forgets the extent to which US government policy was responsible for encouraging increased use of consumer credit. Indeed if any one institution is to blame for eroding what one report pointed out was the "pious, sober, hardworking, and disciplined" nature of the average American person,[21] it was the government for assuming credit use should be the correct route to future US prosperity. Welfare policies were a step too close to socialism; pay rises too likely to have their own negative effects on price inflation. Instead more consumer credit was to the answer, and broadly speaking this has never been reversed.

It was only a matter of time after that the future item of choice for the consumer emerged on the scene: the plastic payment card. There's some dispute over where and when the credit card was invented (according to Encyclopedia Britannica, for example, oil companies and hotel chains issued them to their customers; however, there are references without citation in the entry to credit cards circulating in Europe as far back as the 1890s). The Bank of America issued its first credit card in 1958, long before its competitors. In 1966 American Express and MasterCard created their credit cards; Visa would introduce theirs in 1970. Meanwhile other companies were in on the act. William Barron Hilton I of Hilton Hotels started the Carte Blanche credit card in 1959, losing $2m before selling the credit card business up to Citibank six years later, while the Diners' Club would allow cashless transactions in its restaurants in 1961.

Naturally, of course, these means of consumer credit were still very much out of the reach of most American families. It wasn't until the 1980s that credit cards became something for (nearly) everyone. In 1983, 37 percent of American families had a credit card. Come 1992, 62 percent of US households had at least one card. By 2004, 72 percent of US households had a credit card.[22] The price paid for replacing wider welfare policies with consumer credit access was that 17 percent of people with incomes below the poverty line had a credit card in 1983, rising to 36.2 percent in 1995. The magnitude of credit card debts in poor households increased from 18 percent in 1983 to 39.1 percent in 1995. From 1989 to 2001, the proportion of US households in bottom income quintile (poorest 20 percent) with credit cards went from 29.3 to 42.9 percent.[23] By 2004, 47.9 percent of US families had some kind of debt secured by residential property, 46 percent had some kind of installment debt, and 46.2 percent had some kind of credit card debt. In some way 76 percent of all Americans were indebted.[24]

The loan shark and the salary lenders

When we think of loan sharks we may think of criminal gangs or lone usurious individuals who threaten people with baseball bats or break kneecaps. People today may even think of the mob or, to use a well-known example from popular culture, *The Sopranos*. But this was not always the case. As Robert Mayer has pointed out, the loan shark was not always a mobster. Often they were suited individuals who loitered around offices and factories referring to themselves as salary brokers or salary lenders. The name loan shark is assumed to have derived from the land shark, a name for unscrupulous traders who lurked around ports in nineteenth-century America. It is thought that the first mention of the loan shark was made in an 1888 copy of the Chicago Tribune in an article about the conditions of Minnesota farmers who were victims of rip-off moneylenders.[25] As opposed to the alternative nom de guerre "loan spiders," the term loan shark seemed to stick and was from then on used to refer to urban, as well as rural, lenders. Because of the perceived ease with which a loan shark could operate in Chicago, referred to by the sociologist and historian Earle Eubank as the safest and most liberal city in the United States for the predatory lenders, they had also come to be known as South Clark Street Condors.

In an argument that is as familiar now as it was back in the early 1900s, The Chicago Times often waxed lyrical against public sector employees getting paid more for the same work as private sector employees. Back then, however, these wages were often delayed. When councils could not afford to pay its employees the correct sums of money it would issue them a scrip, or substitute for legal tender, which were not redeemable from banks. Being immediately excluded from mainstream financial services, council employees would have to seek refuge from the only operators willing to deal with them. Loan sharks would buy these scrips at a discount of between 15 and 30 percent and redeem the paper later.[26] Think of it as an early form of check cashing. Indeed for a loan shark, targeting the poor, who were for the most part financially excluded, made for very lucrative work. Robert Mayer asks us to suppose that a man earns $20 per week. Suppose, for example, that his partner has a child, the cost of having that child delivered is around $100. With no health insurance or a welfare state to turn to in such times there is only the loan shark left to turn to.[27]

Also as old as the loan shark is the moralism that public officials used to character-profile those who were left into the arms of predatory lenders. Mayer makes note of one Chicago police commander who opined that "the racetrack has been the chief cause of the loan shark trouble… there was no reason for a man earning $1000 a year to be without money. He earns enough to have a home." To counter this logic by the commander, one loan shark operating in New York City, cited by the historian of the early salary lenders Clarence Wassam, guessed that three-quarters of his customers were "family men with legitimate needs," while only a quarter were "profligate." During his study, Wassam was able to look at the file of a loan shark in NYC. The typical debtor was a man in his twenties or thirties, married, earning between $51 and 75 per month, and lower middle class.[28] It is of no surprise, of course, to learn that the working poor, over their head in debt, is no new category.

Salary lending, referred also to "five for six" lenders on account of their selling five dollars credit at the start of the week in return for six back as repayment, began as a recognized trade sometime after the civil war. There were no references to salary lending in the press until around the 1890s. In 1907 there were 125 small loan firms running in Chicago and in that same year The Chicago Tribune estimated the loan volume for the industry at around the $25m mark. One in five adults (200,000) trapped with what the Tribune referred to as the "loan octopus"—another name that didn't catch on, but which may adequately describe the stranglehold on which the industry had on its customers. Interestingly, to bust one commonly made myth, one file in the Chicago Tribune's Anti-Loan Shark Bureau "revealed an absence of Jews, both from ranks of borrowers and lenders in chattel mortgage and salary loan transactions."[29] These lenders, much like the payday lenders of the future, would cash a postdated check and charge a fee for each day the check was not negotiated.[30]

The very same risks are present in this form of loan, too. For example, one major concern at the time was the frequency at which a borrower would take cash from a network of different lenders, find himself unable to service particular loans, with companies or impatient individuals largely uninterested in setting up formal debt repayment plans, then get themselves into a great deal of trouble. Such was the reality of an industry that not only didn't talk to itself or, for that matter, encourage prudence, but relied on as little information as possible to bring ease of transaction—which was far more of a priority than how the transaction would affect the debtor. Of course, not knowing to how money borrowers a debtor was in hock to would seem like a very precarious means of living, particularly for a lender lending money secured by an assignment of a wage packet, but they had it no other way in the industry of dangerous debt.

In response to the worrying growth of salary lending the Republican governor Frank Lowden signed the Illinois Small Loan Law, which in turn was modeled on the Uniform Small Loan Law (USLL) in June 1917. From that time on it would be known as the Loan Shark Act.[31] The act seemed to gain traction very early on; just weeks after its implementation a loan shark named Stokes was prosecuted in Chicago. At the same time as the USLL was being hailed as "one of America's greatest advances in social legislation," the New York Times during an 1917 editorial, in a move that can only be described as rather too hasty by half, noted that "Shylocks Have Practically Been Exterminated."[32] This was back in the day that loan sharks were charging 10 percent on loans, such as Stokes. Fast-forward to April 1961 and the "juice men"—who in the words of David E. Scheim would squeeze you "until there's no juice left"[33]—were taking 20 percent a week from their customers. The notorious loan shark mobs in Chicago were led by Sam DeStefano. From gangland thug in the early twenties through to the fifties whereupon he found the economic value of operating as a loan shark, using stolen cash, by the sixties he was leading in his odious field, respected and feared. While he did business with politicians and lawyers, selling them small loans, he also happily accepted the custom of high-risk individuals—the reason being, not too dissimilar from the criticisms of subprime lenders today, that they would provide return custom. However, DeStefano's method of debt collection bears no comparison to anything carried out by legitimate lenders: some have reported on the existence of a sound-proof torture chamber in the basement of his massive Chicago apartment,[34] while others have noted his use of ice picks, cattle prods, blow torches, baseball bats, knives, and hot radiators,[35] before he died in 1973 while awaiting trial for murder.

The flourishing of a formalized industry

When we talk about loan sharking, it must be remembered that the difference between the legal and the illegal, in this context, is licensing, today as well as historically. Predatory lending can be a crime carried out by legal and illegal entities, licensed or unlicensed. Predatory loans can simply be defined as loans that cause more harm than benefit (where result is possibly refinancing, etc.); harmful rent-seeking (where the price may reflect higher risk but when lenders "exert market power to charge higher than competitive rates"); fraud and deceptive practices; other forms of willful nontransparency that don't count as fraud; subprime home loans that waive meaningful legal redress; exploitative collections on loan payments; and discrimination (or targeting).[36] What typified credit, even as it became more widely used, with even more lenders in the market, was the growth and legal acceptance of operators who would very often indulge in predatory lending.

Back in 1878, one Frank J Mackay realized that there was a lot of money to be made from people with modest incomes—a realization that was to influence many businesses for years to come. It is recognized that Mackay was the first inventor and popularizer of the installment loan in 1895. His company, Household Finance Corp, went public after he moved to that epicenter of unsecured lending Chicago. Like many of the other businesses that learned his lessons, the company was not later without its controversies as it became bigger. In the 1960s Mackay moved the company to providing larger, more successful personal loan products, but after hiring William Aldinger in the 1970s, a new chief executive outside of their own senior ranks, formerly of Wells Fargo, he moved the company back to what was described by Jeff Bailey at the Wall Street Journal as "lunchpail lending," providing small-dollar loans to those with limited means.[37] Gary Rivlin in his book *Broke USA* also points out how Household Finance dealt in noxious subprime mortgage lending in the 1980s, expanding out to the working poor and struggling middle classes seeking to get on the property ladder by any means possible. In 1981 it would become Household International Inc., and acquired Beneficial Corporation, its best known competitor in the market, in 1998, made tracks in the United States, Canada, and the United Kingdom, but clearly not content with this growth (or, indeed, perhaps this says a lot about the ways in which credit companies grow at all) was caught up in scandal and made a settlement payment of $486m in 2002 on the charge of predatory lending by attorneys in 46 states.[38] And what happens to finance companies with stains on their records? They were bought out one month after settling in court and in November 2002 HSBC announced the acquisition of the company for $15,294.06m.

As already mentioned 34 states adopted a version of the Uniform Small Loan Law or some equivalent. It is noted that the interest rate cap varied over the course of around half a dozen incarnations of the law, though in general it ranged from between 3 and 3.5 percent per month, which is the equivalent to between 36 and 42 percent per year. Today in many jurisdictions 36 percent interest is still the benchmark from which to work. Either states have moved to get rid of rate caps altogether, while others have been more flexible and responsive to the views of the payday lending industry. A few states have gone so far as making interest rate ceilings so low that it is almost impossible for a lender to operate at all.

However, aside from the various ways and means found to regulate credit, something that, in hindsight, might be described as the making of the payday lending industry started to form in the early 1980s. Felt to be the outcome of the Depository Institutions Deregulation and Monetary Control Act in 1980, which was a reaction by the federal government to the rise in inflation, existing state and local usury laws were effectively rendered nullified, giving way to the elimination of interest rate limits.[39] Deregulation after the 1980s also enticed many banks to eliminate what was considered "money-losing" activity and services such as small consumer loans, which there was still a demand for in the market. Lawsuits such as Anderson v H&R Block, Inc. in which it was hoped that tax refund anticipation loans (loans made, as the name implies, in anticipation of a tax refund) violated state usury laws in Alabama showed that the fine print of the National Bank Act overrode a state's claim of usury against a national bank. In 1978 the case of the Marquette National Bank of Minneapolis vs. First of Omaha Service Corp., ruled that state anti-usury laws could not enforce against nationally chartered banks in other states. This decision upheld the constitutionality of the National Bank Act, permitting chartered banks to charge their highest home-state interest rates in any state in which they operated. There was to be in the years after that decision an explosion in consumer credit, but a fallback for predatory lenders lending short-term loans at above reasonable interest, according to state laws, could partner with national banks in order to keep lending legally according to ruling.

With this rather helpful gift to predatory lending it is no surprise to learn that only a few years later the formalization of short-term credit for the working poor re-emerged—though of course many would rightly argue that it never really went away. As Gary Rivlin demonstrates, making money from the impoverished working poor, in its new guise of cash advances for the so-called ALICE customers (asset limited, income constrained, employed), really started in 1983 in Irving, Texas, with Jack Daugherty who set up Cash America as a single pawnshop, then sitting on the Cash America International board of directors since its beginnings in 1984. The company, which operates today as QuickQuid in the UK, DollarsDirect Canada, DollarsDirect Australia, and Cash America Mexico, as well as Cash America and CashNetUSA, was the first to realize the potential profits from serving the under-banked, and one of the first to offer a payday loan type product; the evidence of this being that within four years of operating, first as one store, then as a wide network of stores, sold five million shares for $14.6m and acquired Big State Pawn chain of 47 pawnshops.[40] Before long small-dollar lending caught on in an irreversible way. It was realized by check cashing firms in the early 1990s that additional profits could be made if advance cash was extended to customers rather than just cashing checks. This also provided an incentive to circumnavigate the laws, which while explicit on paper were seldom enforced. Firms hoped that they could avoid credit laws if they labeled their services as check cashing rather than loans. In a bid to avoid usury laws loans could also be referred to as deferred presentment. This clear and present skirting around regulation paid off in more ways than one. Come 1998 some 19 states had a specific law permitting payday lending, 13 states allowed it under their existing small loan laws, while only 18 had small loan laws which effectively prohibited payday lending.[41]

Even in these states the relative slowness of the regulators to get up to speed with issues still quite new to them, particularly when lenders were defining and redefining themselves to buckle regulatory efforts, meant huge delays in determining whether a particular moneylender would have to submit to state small loan laws. On the back of the growing acceptance of the industry, and its ability to run rings around officials, its major part in the financial sector, in the United States and beyond, was set in stone forever. Check Into Cash, widely accepted as the first operation to which the term payday lending can genuinely be ascribed, opened in 1993 and the face of working people's access to personal finance changed beyond repair.

Gary Rivlin refers to an article in the Associated Press that tells of a woman called Janet Delaney, a hospital food worker on a very modest income, who borrows $200 from Check Into Cash after falling behind on bills. After one year Delaney has paid back almost $1000 in fees but not the original $200 principal. In the very same article Allan Jones is quoted as saying: "I'm just lucky. I hit on something that's very popular with consumers." Jones in the same article also notes that people are willing to pay for convenience. That is often the cited reason, particularly by the industry itself, for why the payday loan product grew so popular, so quickly. Banks were not only unwilling to lend money to a certain type of person anymore—which in turn created the need for the Community Reinvestment Act, more on which in a moment—but also consumers were unwilling to be patient any longer with consumer services by mainstream banks. After all the beginning of the nineties was known to be the start of an instant gratification society—we have fast food, we now want fast cash. But this clearly ignores the real genius, if we can call it that, of the industry.

One influential paper by Flannery and Samolyk[42] addresses the question of whether payday lenders can have the ability to carry out short-term loans, or occasional credit, and survive if there are fewer high-frequency borrowers. Their answer is that it might, but its long-term scale would be substantially decreased. The incentive for this industry, then, is to keep high-frequency borrowers borrowing. This is exemplified in the example of Janet Delaney who drew more revenue for Check Into Cash through rolling over on loans and paying enormous sums in fees rather than someone who borrows a small amount and pays back on time.

Allan Jones cheerily told the Associated Press of how he could "get people in and out [his shops] in thirty seconds." Possibly this was one appeal of payday lending, but it doesn't really get to the heart of why payday lending grew so popular in such a small amount of time. To answer this question we have to ask ourselves which customer type is the payday lending industry in such demand for. Is it the impatient, relatively better-off consumer who doesn't want to visit the bank manager to justify an expense, wants few questions asked, and perhaps wants to keep the bank manager at bay so they can be relied on at a later date (perhaps for a conversation about a mortgage loan)? Or is it the working poor consumer who has seen the cost of living increase far faster than their wage packet? As is the case of most financial institutions, for reasons related to image it would be far better for the payday lending industry to communicate to a wider public that it was more popular with the former type of customer. But take the example of a full-time worker at Wal-Mart, raised for example by Rivlin, the largest private employer in the United States, who earns around $16,000 and is trying to lead a decent standard of living. That worker was among the bottom 40 percent of workers by income, whose wages flat-lined on average throughout the 1990s, while, as Rivlin says, "the cost of everything from health care, heating oil, and housing soared." It so happens that this customer is more profitable to payday lenders as well, and this was known early on.

A very useful resource for understanding the different customer type of the formalized payday lending industry was carried out by the UK consumer advocacy group Consumer Focus in 2010 which identifies three character types of a payday loan user: those who had a long-term negative experience from their loan; those who had a mixed short-term experience; and those who had a short-term positive experience.

Those who had a long-term negative experience tended to take out loans and defer payments, thereby extending the life—and repayments—of the loan. They were often lower income earners, had poor credit ratings, viewed short-term finance solutions as the only way of getting extra money, had previous negative experiences with mainstream forms of credit and felt initially positive about the relative lack of enquiry about a loan than would otherwise be experienced trying to take a personal loan out from a bank. How their negative experience played out, whether by having to rollover on existing loans, or forego other necessities in order to pay down debts, is varied.

The short-term mixed experience group, on the other hand, had typically taken only one loan out in the last 12 months, had managed to pay it back on time, but still had reservations about it. This type of borrower also tended to have a low income, few savings, some with existing debts, and the reason they needed a loan was due to a small financial shock such as a later than anticipated payday or unexpected utility bill. Along with expecting banks to turn them away, they also did not want to even deal with banks, as they felt poorly treated during previous meetings.

The short-term positive experience was as to be expected, using the loan as a one-off, paid back in the allocated time frame and benefitting from the relative anonymity of the transaction. This type of borrower also had few savings, but unlike the others, chose to use this type of loan so as not to impact negatively upon getting a larger loan at another time.[43]

Nobody can deny the existence of all three types of payday loan user—and the same can be said for when the industry started back in the early 1990s. But what does bear out in the evidence (as we shall see in further discussions) is that one of these three types, in order to meet high levels of profit, which the payday lending sector achieved right from the get-go, was necessary far more than any of the others. It was these people, rather than the better-off one-time user of payday loans, that meant that by 1999, six years after the first Check Into Cash store opened, Allan Jones and Billy Webster, one of the cofounders of Advance America, had seven stores apiece in Dayton, Ohio, alone (where Gary Rivlin has called "Subprime City").

So, what explains the quick success of the industry? Clearly what happened was that the crisis in the cost of living in the early 1990s happened to coincide with the growth of an industry that not only seemed unconcerned by a borrower's ability to pay back money, but also made more money for that reason. For that the industry needed a custom base to reflect the type aligned with the above-mentioned long-term negative experience. Fortunately for the industry, the mainstream finance sector was largely unconcerned by this because as far as it was concerned the people turning up outside payday loans stores were not for them anyway. Early players like Check Into Cash took lessons from the early salary lenders, pawnbrokers, and check cashing joints, but ultimately grew off the back of a toxic mix of the soaring rise in the number of working poor citizens in the United States and the rollback of mainstream finance in certain, poorer communities.

The regulation rat race

Capitalizing on the confusion that the new payday loan product set for regulators, they turned up in places like Oregon, Colorado, and Virginia, then in Wisconsin and Kansas,[44] almost without knowledge. Indeed where laws were too restrictive, payday lenders operated as agents for banks with applications being carried out in a lenders' office while a bank out of state approves and books the loan.[45] The extent to which banks accommodated for payday lenders in some states was demonstrated by

Mann and Hawkins[46] who point out that Wells Fargo provided funding for Advance America, Cash America, and ACE Cash Express, and Bank of America and Wachovia provided a syndicated credit line to Advance America. Furthermore, JPMorgan and Bank of America both own more than 1 percent of CashAmerica.

Salary lending as a precursor to payday lending took off to a degree; however, the experiment of postdated check cashing needed a whole host of external realities to occur before it could really flourish. Increased use of consumer credit as a social and financial norm, lower wages, looser or generally more confused regulation, and, importantly, more of the working poor.

The earliest use of the word payday loan was found by Robert Mayer in an advert for Mr Money, based in Kansas City dealing in postdated checks, in the Atchison (Kansas) Globe and had not just a specific class as target, but race, too; in the nineties, for example, it was found that twice as many check cashers operated in black areas than in white, and also near army living quarters.[47] Similarly pawnbroking has always had a presence in US neighborhoods. Pawnbroking is widely considered the oldest form of consumer lending, existing in China around 2,000–3,000 years ago. The connection between pawning and America has been sustained by the myth that Queen Isabella pawned her jewels to raise funds for Christopher Columbus' first journey. Pawn shops may have been dubbed the "poor man's bank," particularly from around the early 1800s when they turned up on the scene in the United States, but they have previously enjoyed far greater legitimacy. As Dr Robert Johnson points out in his research on the industry, pawnshops[48] were always traditionally family-owned businesses that provided a decent service to those without access to the forms of finance primarily enjoyed only by businesses or the very wealthy in society; however, now their existence provides evidence of a community's poverty.

Dr Johnson doesn't deny the existence of the rogue pawn industry but does point out that, with regard to regulation, the industry was largely compliant. As time went on state regulation of pawnbroking would usually be covered by uniform small lending laws. But as pawnbroking grew larger as an industry, with not just family-owned businesses, but larger enterprises, it became a different beast in general and part of what Gary Rivlin calls Poverty Inc. The provision of small, quick, short-term loans on a vast scale was what the payday lending industry would eventually come to emulate from pawning.

Over time not only has different forms of consumer credit had to understand both the customer it wanted to appeal to, and the kind of lending environment it was operating within, the regulatory system has had to catch up with it. Back in the early 1900s, many businessmen with employees, some of whom were on low incomes, were so fed up with being used as a means to blackmail their staff (as lenders used to intimidate borrowers by threatening to tell their employers and thus risk them being fired as a consequence) that they decided to support uniform small-dollar loan rules in large numbers—if not out of principle then largely on the basis that this would cause them less bother. This, in addition to the growing number of charities who were providing legal support to borrowers who found themselves in trouble with salary lenders, brought about the drafting of the Uniform Small Loan Law with work undertaken by the Russell Sage Foundation.[49]

The Russell Sage Foundation Uniform Small Loan Law came to be defined as having, in 1916, a three-tier approach: (1) higher interest rates for loans of money under a certain amount—as much as 30 or 40 percent; (2) regulated fees and charges; (3) state licensing of lenders. By the 1960s most of that law went into the Uniform Consumer Credit Code, revised in 1974 served as a model for regulation of consumer loans in most states. Additionally, by 1968 the Truth in Lending Act (TILA) came into being as federal law, "designed to promote the informed use of consumer credit, by requiring disclosures about its terms and cost to standardize the manner in which costs associated with borrowing are calculated and disclosed."[50]

Then, as now, the Federal Trade Commission (FTC) works to ensure that the nation's markets are efficient and free of practices that might harm consumers. The motivation for this, of course, is to ensure the smooth operation of the free market system and to ensure the principle that consumers are rational agents, not the deceived subjects of misleading advertising which would, for obvious reasons, not only conflict with the freedom supposedly inherent to a free market capitalist economy, but also the primacy of the individual to make rational decisions in an environment where actors, in this instant credit sellers, are on equal footing under the law and are not wedded to any racket or monopoly—quite contrary to the principles on which the US financial system is based upon.

The FTC, in their interpretation of the Act, and given their duty toward the free consumer, understand that with an omission of vital information or practice that is considered deceptive it is more than likely the result is a misled consumer and may subsequently affect a consumer's behavior or decisions about a given product or service. Importantly the FTC, since the introduction of TILA, has always taken a view on what is considered the fair relationship between a credit seller and a borrower, that's to say an act or practice is considered unfair if the injury it causes, or is likely to cause, is substantial, not outweighed by other benefits, and not reasonably avoidable. Indeed as Christopher Peterson has pointed out, the Small Loan Legislation and Bankruptcy Act of 1898 were the "stepping stones to 'credit revolution,' legitimization of that product, and an end to state sponsored stigma over consumer lending,"[51] the Truth in Lending Act was a sign that state-sponsored stigma was, for the most part, gone (though, of course, not eradicated entirely. Perhaps, it might be argued, its relative disappearance was because the state realized the potential for banks to extend credit to households and the financial rewards that may result) and now focus was placed on the legitimacy of lenders.

TILA was created by noble motivations, the hard task is in regulatory enforcement. The same can also be said of the Community Reinvestment Act (CRA). Again, as Christopher Peterson has pointed out on this topic in 1977 Congress tried to recreate charitable lending as community reinvestment. The CRA was this very outcome, however, "federal regulatory agencies have rarely initiated any action on the basis of a CRA evaluation."[52] The intention of the CRA, signed into law by Jimmy Carter on October 12, 1977, was well needed: it was widely felt at the time that lenders were acting in a prejudiced way when making lending decisions, particularly in some low-income communities and particularly communities where there was a large population of minorities—thus taking on the principles of the Fair Housing Act of 1968 and the Equal Credit Opportunity Act of 1974 which also prohibited discrimination, and the Home Mortgage Disclosure Act of 1975 (HMDA) which obliged banking institutions disclose mortgage lending and application data. This prejudicial practice was referred to as redlining to suggest a process, carried out by financial institutions, to draw a red line around areas it didn't feel it wanted to operate in. The Act very worthily obliges federal agencies to, in turn, encourage regulated financial institutions to assist in meeting the finance needs of the communities in which they operate.

On first glance it looked to be working. By 1984 three of the largest lending institutions, First National Bank of Chicago, Harris Trust and Savings Bank, and the Northern Trust Company, had all committed

$153bn to reinvestment purposes, focusing on single-family and multi-family housing and small business loans. A little while after even the Bank of America had set aside money to the tune of $12bn annually to ensure consumer loans were being lent to lower income families. Allen J. Fishbein in his research on the CRA, looking back 15 years after its inception, remarked that: "Despite the perception by many bankers that lending in low and moderate income areas is too risky and unprofitable, the experience over the last fifteen years has debunked these myths."[53]

For Fishbein the fact that he found numerous examples of successful reinvestment partnerships that demonstrated how lending to residents in urban neighborhoods could be both prudent and indeed profitable for mainstream banking institutions somewhat took the wind out of the criticism that the CRA could not be done. His focus was that lending institutions could in fact meet the needs of low-income communities without bankrupting themselves or engaging in risky lending practices—which itself is written into law, with the CRA actually stating that risky lending be discouraged as part of a lending institution's duty toward CRA ends. The issue, however, was again enforcement. Even at the outset of the inception of the CRA, community groups who volunteered to oversee the enforcement of the CRA found major issues with the way in which regulators supervised banks. In Fishbein's research it was supposed that enforcement was not always quite so rigorous. Agencies were viewed as being too cozy and too protective of the institutions they were supposed to supervise. This created the urgency for reform (which the CRA has been subject to a lot of over the years) and saw Congress amend the act in 1989 in order to force disclosure to the public the results of CRA assessments made periodically and to ensure that the methods of enforcing banks to meet their obligations was fit for purpose. After this, it was noted by Fishbein that between 1990 and 1992 only 939 banks (9.8 percent) were deemed in need of improvement and 87 (0.9 percent) substantially noncompliant out of the 9,520 banks that were covered.[54]

The early 1990s and the newfound focus on banking regulation of the Clinton government was a turning point for the CRA. After 15 years of its passing in Congress, $30bn overall was committed by lenders to poor communities across the United States. According to Richard Marsico at the New York Law School in 1992,[55] a raft of issues including the 1989 Savings and Loan ("S&L") bailout legislation, a wave of bank mergers, the release of 1990 and 1991 Home Mortgage Disclosure Act data which pointed to widespread racial disparities in home mortgage lending, renewed attention on urban poverty, in large part a consequence of the Los Angeles riots in 1992, and Clinton's vision of bank lending as a social policy tool gave strength to the original purpose of the CRA. Marsico mentioned also that strengthening enforcement standards and the billions of dollars in CRA lending commitments, made by banks, is evidence that more efforts to strive for a better CRA is worth it; however, he concludes that in recent time "the CRA is a vague statute that has not been vigorously enforced."

This was the environment into which the payday lending industry entered in 1993—the same year that check cashers cashed a total of $150m worth of checks and charged $700m in fees.[56] While billions had been earmarked by banks toward CRA activity it didn't stop the creation and eventual rise of the payday lending industry—and with looking at the sums that could be charged in fees from relatively little, it is not difficult to see why. It must also be noted that the CRA was and never has been applicable to payday lending; neither, too, was the Truth in Lending Act. It is all well and good having obligations set on lenders, to show that their products are not suitable for everyone, as is the case of the payday loan; however, that matters for very little if the information presented is not registered by consumers. In the conclusion to his book on high-cost credit industry Christopher Peterson points out that in order for Truth in Lending to benefit consumers who are contemplating risky high-cost credit a reasonable understanding of the contract on a Federal Reserve Board high-cost credit application form should be demonstrated. This was in no way supposed to sneer at consumers. Information such as annualized percentage rates is notoriously confusing, not to mention the fact that the loans at issue are short term by their very nature. A demonstration of understanding, in this way, would only determine the extent to which a payday lender had explained their product properly, as well as the associated risks. The rise in dangerously high debt attached to payday lending, from its very inception, was evidence enough that Truth in Lending was not always made good on in the industry—a battle that has been a regular feature for any federal state attempting to properly regulate the industry in subsequent years. Indeed as Peterson also points out TILA "unwittingly facilitated... naivety, by providing all lenders the same veneer of legitimacy."

Right at the time that mainstream banks were supposed to pick up the pace and lend responsibly to low-income communities, to ensure they were not left in to the arms of credit sellers with far less attractive terms, the payday lending industry had formed and developed a product known for its high cost and its associated predatory practices.

From where did the payday lenders emerge?

The growth of the payday lending industry in the United States would be the envy of any other type of business. In 1999 there were around 100,000 outlets across the country.[57] Research carried out by the Consumer Federation of America and the US Public Interest Research Group found that by the end of 2001 between 12,000 and 14,000 payday loan stores made more than 100 loans per month. By 2005 the number of payday outlets across the United States had reached over 200,000 and the industry had risen in loan volume to $40bn. No longer was this merely a small industry filling a gap in the market to a select few unbankable individuals. Certainly this was no industry to be ignored. It grew very quickly into a beast that desperately needed taming.

As Gary Rivlin has found not only did the payday lending industry to begin with find rather genius ways of selling their products to the people it wanted to target, it also managed to shield itself, by and large, from a regulatory system on the back foot. Quoting a man called Jim Higgins, who gave a presentation called "Effective Marketing Strategies to Dominate Your Market" at the Las Vegas payday lenders convention which provides the backbone of Rivlin's book, we start to see what is considered *best practice* as regards to attracting a certain type of clientèle, firstly by sending out "Welcome" mailers, offering good deals on exchanging checks such as "Cash 3, Get 1 Free" on the grounds that "These are people who are not used to getting anything free." While gaining considerable ground targeting the working poor the industry successfully removed any legal impediments for the sector to grow—even in states where usury laws still existed. To show its relative strong growth in its infancy, one paper on usury laws in the United States shows that the industry came about around the same time as Starbucks went on the rise, in 1992 when the coffee company offered the public shares of stock for the first time. Steven Graves and Christopher Peterson demonstrate that the coffee chain's rise has been held as "not unlike the cultural blitz of personal computing," and yet its "growth pales in comparison to the growth of the payday lending outlets in the wake of slackening usury limits."[58]

DOI: 10.1057/9781137361103.0004

Rather counterintuitively, in Graves and Peterson's paper they find in their database of payday lender locations and index on conservative Christian political power that payday lenders tend to concentrate in high densities in conservative Christian states. Indeed were it not for moves in Georgia and North Carolina to outlaw payday lending, just as their research was taking place in 2008, that relationship would have been a lot bolder than it already is. Their research found that of the 30 U.S. House of Representatives districts most saturated with payday lending, 25 (including the top ten) are located within the most conservative Christian states. This of course speaks to the demographic that makes up conservative Christian states. A Gallup poll in January 2014[59] found that six of the 10 poorest states in the United States are also the most conservative (Mississippi, Idaho, Utah, South Carolina, Arkansas, and Alabama). But the impression one gets from the index on conservative Christian political power is that it has historically done the least to try and take control of the growing amount of payday lenders that have cropped up in their neighborhoods.

Other claims by notable academics such as David Graeber, the author of *Debt: The First 5000 Years*,[60] would suggest this isn't so hard to believe after all. Graeber points out that in 365AD St Basil delivered a sermon at Cappadocia where he was particularly "offended by the crass dishonesty by which moneylenders operated; their abuse of Christian fellowship...The man in need comes seeking a friend, the rich man pretends to be one. In fact he's a secret enemy, and everything he says is a lie." Clearly the Christian Church had a lot to say as regards usury, as highlighted by this quote, as well as the objection to lending upon usury to one's brother in Deuteronomy 23:19, but Graeber says the Church later had little to say about feudal dependency. It is possible, thus, to say that the scriptures and early teachings of Christianity relating to usurious moneylending objects to the sorts of debt bondage inherent in such a transaction, but over the years the Christian Church has not been quite so damning, necessarily, of bondage in general. A complete look at this would enter us into a discussion about the Christian views toward slavery, which has compelling arguments on both sides suggesting either that there is a deep historical opposition by the Church to slavery, but on the other side evidence that perhaps the Church did not carry out its duties in practice—both highly contested arguments that it would be ill-advised to discuss in detail here—but the wider point Graeber seems to make is that in spite of the teachings of Christianity, where there is

Christian political power there is a disconnect between, shall we say, theory and practice. The same might be applied to the apparent link between conservative Christian political power in the United States and the tendency to have a more relaxed regulatory architecture overseeing the growth of the payday lending industry.

Interestingly four of the six states deemed to be the most poor in terms of income per capita, and conservative, are in the Bible Belt (Alabama, South Carolina, Arkansas, and Mississippi). In two well-regarded studies of what constitutes the Bible Belt it is recognized, firstly by Wilbur Zelinsky,[61] that it is made up predominantly in the South (while applying the term to some parts of the Midwest as well) while Stephen Tweedie[62] has identified in his research that two belts exist simultaneously, one in more Eastern parts incorporating states from Virginia to Florida (excluding Miami to South Florida), and another that is made up of states from Texas to Mississippi. It was noticed by Brett Williams that one of the only reasons there has been a build-up of productive investment in cities, or what depending on how you look at things not so much productive, but destructive, especially in the American South is to do with high-interest, debt generating businesses. Before it was Visa and MasterCard returning to low-income cities with subprime loans, now the malls are awash with "predatory lenders for the poor."[63]

Judging by the volume of the lenders concentrated in particular areas, namely low-income areas with high areas of deprivation, tells a story about who the industry targets. Indeed as I have shown in the very early days payday lenders were far more open about targeting the ALICE customer (asset limited, income constrained, employed) rather than today where it is better for brand and investment to suggest that is balanced mix of cash-strapped working people from low and middle incomes as well as relatively wealthier customers who choose not to engage with the bank manager or want to keep them happy until such time as a visit entails a larger loan, perhaps for a mortgage. While it is easier today to fact check these claims with evidence, given the attention the industry has received, as well as the research that has been carried out on it, it was a lot more difficult during the genesis of the payday loan product to see exactly where it had emerged from. As John Caskey in his research on the industry points out there are no firm data to document its evolution from 1990 to 1995. Backing up the claim that regulators have historically been on the back foot as regards the payday lending industry, Caskey confirms that during these years there were no state regulatory authorities collecting data on the industry, and even more worrying is the fact that he, during his initial research, relied on leaders in the payday lending industry itself to tell him that between 1993 and 1995 an increasing number of check cashers entered the market.[64]

Caskey, in trying to locate news articles on the specific subject of payday loans as part of the research for his book on fringe finance, the first extended study of the issue, recorded absolutely no news articles before 1996. That means that before this time, three years after the introduction of payday loan as a product distinct from all others in the consumer credit market, there were no news agencies looking into the subject. Over the years, particularly with relatively small industries, media reports are key for regulators to attempt to address its remit and change its regulatory structure to fit. As we know regulation in the industry was, and is, a considerable problem—which may indeed be explained by the lack of attention it received by journalists. Even in 1996 itself, only two articles were recorded by Caskey in his research. In 1999 it was 111.[65] Today it is near impossible to pick up a newspaper without some scandal or other taking center stage. In those crucial early days many payday lenders still functioned, or at least operated out of the offices of, check cashing outlets (CCOs). By 2001 some 10,000 payday lenders nationwide functioned as CCOs with around 4,400 of those belonging to firms that operated 200 or more offices across multiple states. By the end of that year alone, according to the Consumer Federation of America and US Public Interest Research Group, it was found that between 12,000 and 14,000 loan stores made more than 100 loans per month.[66] Caskey cites the work of journalist John Pletz[67] who supposed that the reason pawnbroking as an industry stopped growing between 1992 and 1997 at the fast pace it had gotten used to previously between was because of a stronger economy; however, his analysis failed to recognize the extent to which payday lending was becoming a force to be reckoned with, and will almost certainly be what explains the explosive growth of CCOs between 1998 and 2003.[68]

In the period between 1999 and 2005 the payday lending industry had reportedly risen to the extent where loan volume was $40bn. The average wage packet of the customers using loans was around $25,000, though 23 percent were earning less than this.[69] One study in 2005 found that in North Carolina, one of the first states to explicitly authorize payday lending, there could be found a concentration of customers from African American communities, some of whom were from the most poorest backgrounds. No coincidence, then, to find that North Carolina was a state where payday lenders had grown considerably—having just 307 stores in 1997 to 1,204 in 2001.[70] From Missouri to Washington State, Florida to Texas, Oregon to Louisiana, payday lenders bore witness to yearly growth of hundreds of percent. Millions of loans, millions in fees, and no indication that this was going to get better before it got worse. Fringe banking in the fringe finance industry, where the poor became big business, broke all the rules and got away with it. Today, according to research undertaken by The Pew Charitable Trusts, over 12m Americans use payday lenders each year, which in 2010 saw the loan volume reach $30bn. Though designed to be for one-off use to provide for income shortfalls before payday, two-thirds of loan customers went on to take out seven or more loans after, paying $15–20 on every $100 they borrow—which can end up being around 350 percent in interest for a two week loan. The average borrower takes out eight loans of $375 each per year and spends $520 on interest.[71]

Writing in 2008 Professor Mary Spector of the Southern Methodist University Dedman School of Law, in providing some figures around how many stores from US payday lending companies had opened, highlighted the extent to which what was being bred was an industry with reach way out further than just one country: To name just three companies ACE Cash Express (ACE) had 1500 stores in 38 states, Cash America Intl had 500 pawnshops worldwide, but Dollar Financial Corp had 800 outlets trading as Loan Mart in the United States, Money Mart in Canada, and a further 200 outlets trading as The Money Shop in the UK.[72] In a very quick space of time payday lending went from emulating check cashing outlets and salary lenders in small stores to covering a lot of ground in low-income areas. In yet another short space of time it went on to have publicly listed companies, trade associations, and stores in most US states—the next frontier was global reach.

Notes

1   See, for example, Gelpi, Rosa-Maria and Julien-Labruyère, François (2005), *The History of Consumer Credit: Doctrines and Practice*, UK: Palgrave Macmillan; Hudson, Michael "The New Economic Archaeology of Debt," *Michael Hudson*, April 23, 2002. Available at http://michael-hudson.com/2002/04/the-new-economic-archaeology-of-debt/; and Graeber, David (2011), *Debt: The First 5000 Years*, US: Melville House.

Payday Lending

2 Peterson, Christopher (2004), *Taming the Sharks: Towards a Cure for the High Cost Credit Market*, US: University of Akron Press.
3 Graves, Steven and Peterson, Christopher (2008), Usury Law and the Christian Right: Faith Based Political Power and the Geography of the American Payday Loan Regulation, *Catholic University Law Review*, Vol. 57, p. 637.
4 The Community Reinvestment Association of North Carolina (2001), *Too Much Month at the End of the Paycheck: Payday Lending in North Carolina*, US: The Community Reinvestment Association of North Carolina.
5 Clark, Evans (1930), *Financing the Consumer*, New York: Harper & Bros.
6 Johnson, Dr Robert W. (1998), *Pawnbroking in the US: A Profile of Customers*, Washington: The Credit Research Center.
7 Carruthers, Bruce G. and Ariovich, Laura (2010), *Money and Credit: A Sociological Approach*, US: Polity.
8 Ibid.
9 Hyman, Louis (2011), *Debtor Nation: The History of America in Red Ink*, US: Princeton University Press.
10 Ibid.
11 Ibid.
12 Klassen, Henry C. (1992), T. C. Power & Bro.: The Rise of a Small Western Department Store, 1870–1902, *The Business History Review*, Vol. 66, No. 4, p. 671.
13 Carruthers, Bruce G. and Ariovich, Laura (2010), *Money and Credit: A Sociological Approach*, US: Polity.
14 Ibid.
15 Bolles, John Augustus (2009), *A Treatise on Usury and Usury Laws*, US: University of Michigan Library.
16 See the First Amendment, http://www.law.cornell.edu/constitution/first_amendment.
17 Hyman, Louis (2011), *Debtor Nation: The History of America in Red Ink*, US: Princeton University Press.
18 Ibid.
19 Ibid.
20 Cohen, Lizabeth (2003), *A Consumers' Republic: The Politics of Mass Consumption in Postwar America*, US: Vintage Books.
21 The Community Reinvestment Association of North Carolina (2001), *Too Much Month at the End of the Paycheck: Payday Lending in North Carolina*, US: The Community Reinvestment Association of North Carolina.
22 Bird, Edward J. et al. (1999), Credit Card Debts of the Poor: High and Rising, *Policy Analysis & Management*, Vol. 125.
23 Carruthers, Bruce G. and Ariovich, Laura (2010), *Money and Credit: A Sociological Approach*, US: Polity.
24 Ibid.

25 Mayer, Robert (2010), *Quick Cash: The Story of the Loan Shark*, US: Northern Illinois University Press.
26 Ibid.
27 Ibid.
28 Wassam, Clarence W. (1908), *The Salary Loan Business in New York City*, US: Bureau of Social Research, New York School of Philanthropy.
29 Mayer, Robert (2010), *Quick Cash: The Story of the Loan Shark*, US: Northern Illinois University Press.
30 Caskey, John (2005), Fringe Banking and the Rise of Payday Lending, In Bolton, P. and Rosenthal, H. (eds), *Credit Markets for the Poor*, New York: Russell Sage Foundation.
31 Mayer, Robert (2010), *Quick Cash: The Story of the Loan Shark*, US: Northern Illinois University Press.
32 Ibid.
33 Scheim, David E. (1989), *Contract on America: The Mafia Murder of President John F. Kennedy*, US: Zebra.
34 Dark, Tony (2008), *A Mob of His Own: Samuel Mad Sam DeStefano and the Chicago Mob's Juice Rackets*, Chicago: H.H. Productions.
35 Mayer, Robert (2010), *Quick Cash: The Story of the Loan Shark*, US: Northern Illinois University Press.
36 Engel, Kathleen C. and McCoy, Patricia A. (2006), Predatory Lending and Community Development at Loggerheads, *Cleveland-Marshall Legal Studies*, Paper No. 05-105.
37 Rivlin, Gary (2011), *Broke USA*, US: HarperBusiness.
38 Bray, Chad, HSBC to Appeal $2.46bn Judgment, *New York Times*, October 18, 2013. Available at http://www.nytimes.com/2013/10/19/business/international/hsbc-to-appeal-2-46-billion-judgment.html?_r=0.
39 Flannery, Mark J. and Samolyk, Katherine (2005), Payday Lending: Do the Costs Justify the Price?, *FDIC Center for Financial Research Working Paper*, No. 2005/09.
40 For more information see the history page for Cash America. Available at http://www.cashamerica.com/aboutus/CompanyHistory.aspx.
41 Flannery, Mark J. and Samolyk, Katherine (2005), Payday Lending: Do the Costs Justify the Price?, *FDIC Center for Financial Research Working Paper*, No. 2005/09.
42 Ibid.
43 Burton, Marie (2010), *Keeping the Plates Spinning: Perceptions of Payday Loans in Great Britain*, UK: Consumer Focus. For a further discussion on Burton's findings see Packman, Carl, Loan Sharks (2012): *The Rise and Rise of Payday Lending*, UK: Searching Finance.
44 Mayer, Robert (2010), *Quick Cash: The Story of the Loan Shark*, US: Northern Illinois University Press.

45 Caskey, John (2005), Fringe Banking and the Rise of Payday Lending, In Bolton, P. and Rosenthal, H. (eds), *Credit Markets for the Poor*, New York: Russell Sage Foundation.
46 Mann, Ronald J. and Hawkins, Jim (2007), Just Until Payday, *UCLA Law Review*, Vol. 54.
47 Mayer, Robert (2010), *Quick Cash: The Story of the Loan Shark*, US: Northern Illinois University Press.
48 Johnson, Dr Robert W. (1998), *Pawnbroking in the US: A Profile of Customers*, US: Credit Research Center.
49 Gallert, David et al. (1932), *Small Loan Legislation: A History of the Regulation of Lending Small Sums*, US: Russell Sage Foundation.
50 Dlabay, Les R. et al. (2009), *Intro to Business*, US: Cengage South-Western.
51 Peterson, Christopher (2004), *Taming the Sharks: Towards a Cure for the High Cost Credit Market*, US: University of Akron Press.
52 Ibid.
53 Fishbein, Allen J (1992), The Community Reinvestment Act After Fifteen Years: It Works, but Strengthened Federal Enforcement Is Needed, *Fordham Law Journal*, Vol. 20, No. 2, pp. 298–310.
54 Ibid.
55 Marsico, Richard (1992), A Guide to Enforcing the Community Reinvestment Act, *Fordham Urban Law Journal*, Vol. 20, No. 2, pp. 165–199.
56 Williams, Brett (2005), *Debt for Sale: A Social History of the Credit Trap*, US: University of Pennsylvania Press.
57 pector, Mary (2008), Payday Loans: Unintended Consequences of American Efforts to Tame the Best, In Kelly-Louw, M., Nehf, J., and Rott, P. (eds), *The Future of Consumer Credit Regulation: Creative Approaches to Emerging Problems*, US: Ashgate.
58 Graves, Steven and Peterson, Christopher (2008), Usury Law and the Christian Right: Faith Based Political Power and the Geography of the American Payday Loan Regulation, *Catholic University Law Review*, Vol. 57.
59 Swift, Art, Wyoming Residents Most Conservative, D.C. Most Liberal, *Gallup*, January 31, 2014. Available at http://www.gallup.com/poll/167144/wyoming-residents-conservative-liberal.aspx.
60 Graeber, (2011), *Debt: The First 5000 Years*, US: Melville House.
61 Zelinsky, Wilbur (1961), An Approach to the Religious Geography of the United States: Patterns of Church Membership in 1952, *Annals of the Association of American Geographers*, Vol. 51, No. 2, pp. 139–193.
62 Tweedie, Stephen (1978), Viewing the Bible Belt, *Journal of Popular Culture*, Vol. 11, No. 4, pp. 865–876.
63 Williams, Brett (2005), *Debt for Sale: A Social History of the Credit Trap*, US: University of Pennsylvania Press.

64 Caskey, John (2004), *Fringe Banking: Check-Cashing Outlets, Pawnshops, and the Poor*, New York: Russell Sage Foundation; and Caskey, John (2005), Fringe Banking and the Rise of Payday Lending, In Bolton, P. and Rosenthal, H. (eds), *Credit Markets for the Poor*, New York: Russell Sage Foundation.
65 Caskey, John (2005), Fringe Banking and the Rise of Payday Lending, In Bolton, P. and Rosenthal, H. (eds), *Credit Markets for the Poor*, New York: Russell Sage Foundation.
66 Figure found in Specter, Mary (2008), Payday Loans: Unintended Consequences of American Efforts to Tame the Beast, In Kelly-Louw, M., Nehf, J., and Rott, P. (eds), *The Future of Consumer Credit Regulation: Creative Approaches to Emerging Problems*, US: Ashgate.
67 Pletz, John, Strong Economy Makes Business Difficult for Pawnshops, *Austin American-Statesman*, August 24, 1999.
68 Caskey, John (2005), Fringe Banking and the Rise of Payday Lending, In Bolton, P. and Rosenthal, H. (eds), *Credit Markets for the Poor*, New York Russell Sage Foundation.
69 Specter, Mary (2008), Payday Loans: Unintended Consequences of American Efforts to Tame the Beast, In Kelly-Louw, M., Nehf, J., and Rott, P. (eds), *The Future of Consumer Credit Regulation: Creative Approaches to Emerging Problems*, US: Ashgate.
70 Caskey, John (2005), Fringe Banking and the Rise of Payday Lending, In Bolton, P. and Rosenthal, H. (eds), *Credit Markets for the Poor*, New York: Russell Sage Foundation.
71 The Pew Charitable Trusts (2012), *Payday Lending in America: Who Borrows, Where They Borrow, and Why*, US: The Pew Charitable Trusts.
72 Specter, Mary (2008), Payday Loans: Unintended Consequences of American Efforts to Tame the Beast, In Kelly-Louw, M., Nehf, J., and Rott, P. (eds), *The Future of Consumer Credit Regulation: Creative Approaches to Emerging Problems*, US: Ashgate.

2
Payday in the UK

Abstract: *The chapter on the UK looks at the historical development of regulation over consumer credit before addressing the issue of financial inclusion. It looks at the impact of a highly indebted population in a country hit by recession, at the growth of payday lending, particularly from US companies, and at the buildup of alternative, ethical finance from credit unions to CDFIs.*

Keywords: consumer credit; credit unions; debt; financial inclusion; ethical finance

Packman, Carl. *Payday Lending: Global Growth of the High-Cost Credit Market.* New York: Palgrave MacMillan, 2014. DOI: 10.1057/9781137361103.0005.

The UK has had a high-cost credit industry for as long as the US. It can be said for certain that the UK has had a payday lending industry for as long, too. Of course pawnbroking has existed in the UK for as long as history can recall. Many households today in the UK will be familiar with the Provident, or the "provvy," who have been supplying working class households with short-term cash loans since 1880.[1] Cash checking in the UK is equally as familiar as it is in the US. DFC Global Corp, a large US company whose most profitable companies are abroad, has one of its most profitable operations in the UK in The Money Shop, a subsidiary of Dollar Financial UK Limited, cashing checks since 1992. In 2009, The Money Shop was recorded as having 273 stores and 64 franchises across the UK, with ambitions to holding 1,200 stores in the future,[2] as well as a strong online base through its 2011 acquisition of PayDay UK, one of Britain's biggest online payday lending outlets.

A very telling article popped up in 2011 in the *Financial Times*—the UK's foremost news outlet for business and economics—that spoke volumes about the extent to which the UK had become a host body for the US' payday lending industry: "Every day for a week, they rode buses and tubes to parts of the city most visitors would only end up in by mistake, places like Barking, Ilford, Kilburn and Wood Green." The payday lending hopefuls, representatives of the company Speedy Cash which is part of Speedy Cash Holdings Corp., dealing in cash advance loans in the US since 1997, were looking, as they said themselves, "Anywhere that wasn't Westminster or Chelsea or Richmond."[3]

Essentially it shows that executives from a profitable US payday loans company were looking to set up shop in the parts of London that have traditionally been low-paid areas. Indeed when the recession hit in 2008, Kilburn, in the northwest of London, was noted by the BBC as the face of UK financial downturn. In 2013 it was the area focused on by the campaigning group Movement For Change, an influential grouping of people, the outcome of an idea of David Miliband, the unsuccessful contestant of the leadership bid of the UK Labour Party, that took on the issue of payday lending as its own, running the Kilburn Fair Credit Commission to highlight community work carried out expressly to highlight the wrongs committed by the payday lending industry.

But why did those executives choose London and the UK over the many countries between them open to the high-cost credit industry? The answer can be found in looking at the evolution of the regulatory system of the UK with regards to consumer credit.

The development of regulation over consumer credit

The history of consumer credit regulation in the UK can be described fairly as oscillating irregularly from light-touch to overcomplicated. The Pawnbroking Act of 1872 was made on the realization that licensed pawnbrokers and their customers, the owners of property pledged, were not always protected.[4] Before then it had been noted that laws regarding pawnbroking, such as the Pawnbroker's license law 1785, benefited borrowers more than lenders (despite the fact that pawnbrokers for a long time raised a toast to John Scott, the 1st Earl of Eldon, for his part in the modern history of pawnbroking regulation after 1800, an area close to his heart given the frequency with which he himself visited pawnbrokers); so it was seen in large part as a corrective that the 1872 Act returned the benefit to pawnbrokers themselves. Rather interestingly, the Select Committee which came to oversee the realization of the 1872 Act did not hear from any customers in its call for evidence, but was assured by Dudley Ryder, the 2nd Earl of Harrowby, who under Lord Palmerston was Chancellor of the Duchy of Lancaster in 1855, that the "Bill had met with the approbation of city missionaries and other friends of the poor"—which was as much as the poor could ask for at the time.

The 1872 Act limited pawnbrokers' advances to £10.00 in a single transaction, after which a moneylender's license would be required—which given that most pawnbroking was carried out on the basis of sums as little as £2.00 was seldom a consideration. By the time of the Moneylenders Act of 1900, however, it was probably worth considering. The Act was very light-touch, requiring lenders to purchase licenses at minimal costs of £1.00 for three years, or 6 shillings and 8 pence per annum.[5] Purchasing a license came with no examination by authorities, or assessment of the suitability of the candidate. Protections for borrowers were thin with no clear steer on the amount of interest a lender could charge. During a Select Committee hearing in 1898 it was heard from one moneylender who admitted to charging over 3,000 percent in interest.[6] One small favorable element for the borrower was the notion of "harsh and unconscionable," a legal turn of phrase by which a Court of law could measure whether demands of a lender were deemed excessive. If it was found that the terms of a loan from a moneylender were "harsh and unconscionable," then the Court could find in the borrower's favor, but the definition of the legal term was so loose, and the legal process so costly, that often lenders could sidestep the law. After the passing of the Moneylenders Act of 1927 the interest of any loan by a moneylender could not exceed 48 percent; however, as Damon Gibbons has pointed out enforcement of the law was difficult because the formula to calculate the interest rate was so complex and that it required borrowers to take unscrupulous lenders to court[7]—running into the same problems as the Act that preceded it. Indeed in a 1966 discussion about the differences in the Moneylenders Act rate formula and true rate of interest by M.T.L. Bizley, he notes that "experience has shown that even when the layman is aware that the formula does not tell him the true rate, he is often unable to calculate the latter and is uncertain as to whether the Act overstates or understates it."[8]

In 1965, the Crowther Committee was established to extend laws over consumer credit more broadly rather than just the bills of sale and moneylending. Their first report was published in 1971, which pointed out that previous laws were so confused that it would be far easier and simpler to start again rather than amend existing laws. While the plans were perceived as mostly positive by the Conservative government, led by Edward Heath, the Department of Trade and Industry initially did nothing about it. It was only after 1973 that a white paper entitled Reform of the Law on Consumer Credit was published planning to implement all the recommendations in the initial Crowther Committee report. The Consumer Credit Act of 1974 abolished seven previous laws on consumer credit in their entirety, including the Moneylenders Act of 1927 and the Pawnbrokers Act of 1872, and replaced them with a single overarching framework. One exception not eventually taken on by the government was the price of credit, where in the Crowther report it pointed out that "less educated and poorer members of the community...are frequently in the position of paying higher interest rates than are justified by their relative creditworthiness."[9] Despite finding that standard "moneylender" loans were between 30 and 50 percent, with the average loan being around 40 percent, Crowther neglected to define what he meant by "grossly exorbitant" interest and the government was reluctant to go as far as to address what this could mean—particularly so close to an election.

In repealing the many existing laws, under which consumer credit would normally have been addressed, and avoiding commitments to provide cost caps, from 1974 the UK has not had an interest rate ceiling. Interestingly, in the 1970s, during a period of negative after-tax real interest rates, the UK attempted to control credit with stringent measures such as liquidity ratios on banks, special deposits (the "corset"), regulations on minimum deposits and maximum repayment periods on hire purchase credit, and directives and persuasion aimed at building societies to limit lending and/or to keep nominal interest rates low.[10] In the 1980s, the Thatcher government took a different direction entirely, abolishing controls, including the "corset"; the economic policy was marked out by 1986 for its "Big Bang," the pursuit of deregulation in the financial markets that arguably resulted in the spurring on some of the effects of the global financial crisis of 2007–2012.[11] By 1979, however, the amount of outstanding consumer credit advanced by banks was little under £5bn, but by 1986 that figure was £24.2bn. In 1990 it had reached £67bn. The UK was one of the most indebted countries in Europe. Money owed on credit cards in 1971, when there was only the one option through Barclaycard, was £32m; fast-forward to 2009 and the figure was £25bn.

The need for financial inclusion

Through a time of increasing indebtedness, and the realization that low-income communities were often excluded from mainstream finance, finding themselves at the beck and call of predatory lenders in the form of short-term high-cost personal lenders, both legal and illegal, and paying the most for their credit, the UK government began to explore the concept of financial inclusion as a means of countering the inevitable turn in an economy so wedded to debt. In 1998 policy action teams (PAT) were set up to try and find policy points and actions to try and tackle the variety of ways people were socially excluded in the UK. In 1999 policy action team 14 (PAT 14), who had been looking specifically at financial exclusion, came to recommend the creation of basic bank accounts.[12] Additionally the team recommended the use and retention of the following:

- an appropriate account, or equivalent product, into which income is paid, can be held securely and accessed easily;
- an appropriate method of paying, and spreading the cost of, household bills and other regular commitments;
- an appropriate method of paying for goods and services, including making remote purchases by telephone and on the Internet;
- an appropriate means to smooth income and expenditure.[13]

The minimum wage should provide an adequate standard of living and general taxation should provide

- adequate income replacement in cases of job loss, disability, or ill health;
- an adequate minimum income in old age that is not means-tested;
- a safety net of interest-free loans and grants for people on very low incomes who need to meet a major expense or to cover major expenditure in a crisis;
- free health and dental care at the point of use.

To help individuals meet periodic needs, our vision is that there should be

- sustainable lower-cost alternatives to commercial sub-prime lenders;
- savings accounts that are secure, are accessible, and protect savings from inflation;
- a promotion of regular saving and its material and psychological benefits;
- universal access to basic, appropriate, and affordable home contents insurance;
- free-to-client budgeting and debt advice services.

The Financial Inclusion Taskforce was set up in 2005, which reported to the UK Treasury. The context of its arrival is significant. The Department for Trade and Industry (DTI) in 2004 had just lent its backing to a report that said leveling interest rate ceilings, as had been the case historically, would in turn see large swathes of low-income households turn to illegal lenders instead. Gerry Sutcliffe, the then consumer minister, said: "Ceilings can often have a negative effect, such as excluding low-income consumers from the market or leading them to use [inappropriate] products." The research that Sutcliffe was referring to had been carried out by the independent research group Policis. In their report they pointed out that while it is true France, Germany, and Ireland have caps on their rates of interest to protect consumers, the result has left many families without access to legal credit and has seen them in hock to the black market. These conclusions came under immediate fire. Professor Udo Reifner for example, someone particularly familiar with the European outlook on interest rate restrictions,[14] pointed out that the Policis research misunderstood the very basics of French and German regulation which equipped their banks a monopoly over the advance of consumer credit, the vast majority of which was made available in the form of overdrafts which were widely available.[15] In supposing that it is price caps on the cost of credit which limits access to credit for low-income households, not the monopoly of banks, it has meant that Policis wrongfully assumes that it is the lack of price cap that, in their own words, exerts "downward pressure on price"—despite there being no evidence whatsoever for this.

(Other critics have supposed that this wrongful assumption was perhaps willfully composed. It was noticed by the Consumer Action Law Centre in Australia that Policis had a history of producing research in favor of the high-cost credit market. In 2008 for example, Cash Converters admitted that they had commissioned Policis to produce consumer research on the habits and use of credit by low-income Australians.)

It would be wrong, however, to say this was a step back for the financial inclusion agenda, which was far less about using the state apparatus to limit the influence of the credit industry, and more about long-term methods of financial resilience, one example of which was to encourage lenders in the market to proactively design banking and credit products suitable for low-income households. After the taskforce had finished its work in 2011, it boasted a number of victories including halving the number of people in households without a transaction bank account, the Department for Work and Pension's Growth Fund which provided low-cost credit to financially vulnerable communities, increasing the number of debt advice agencies, and introducing the Savings Gateway, a scheme to get people saving who may not have usually done so.

After the term was coined in 1993,[16] the first major study of financial exclusion in the UK carried out in 1999 by academics at the University of Bristol's Personal Finance Research Centre found that 7 percent of households lacked any mainstream financial products. This research was conducted in addition to a relatively substantial amount of similar work focusing on the financial capabilities of low-income households.[17] Time has shown the government's intervention in this area to be largely positive. An estimate of financial exclusion, based on 2003 data looked at by the European Commission in 2008, indicated that 6 percent of adults in the UK did not have any type of bank account, any form of savings products, or any revolving credit, while a 2009/10 Family Resources Survey found that 5 percent of households and 7 percent of adults lacked any form of savings or a bank account.[18]

However, the recession had a devastating effect on the nation's finances as a whole, on low-income households who were already the more vulnerable, in general. Around one in five of the population said they would have to borrow money if they needed £200 at short notice—either through a formal loan (credit card, overdraft, loan, etc.) or through an informal loan from family/friends.[19] While the most common sources of unsecured credit have historically been through credit cards, bank overdrafts, and personal loans, a worrying development by way of nonmainstream finance in the form of doorstep credit, pawnbroking, and payday lending had taken effect, with the latter of the three being the fastest growing. Despite the best efforts of the Labour government of 1997–2010 to introduce a focus on financial inclusion, the economy as a whole was working in the opposite way, seeing banks rein in services to low-income communities rather than show demonstrable support for inclusion, while all the time personal debt continued to rise.

The recession, the rise of the over-indebted, and the supply of payday loans

In 2013 personal debt shot to an all time high of £1.4tn. A large proportion of this was mortgage debt and thus considered investment, but the rise of debt on account of unsecured lending, borrowing not so much on the promise of relative future prosperity, but to supplement wages and afford to live throughout the month, has been the single most telling sign of economy bonded to dangerous debt. Unsecured consumer debt almost tripled from the early 1990s to the early 2010s, reaching £160.6bn at the end of May 2014. Indebted households in the poorest 10 percent of the UK have average debts more than four times their annual income.[20] Research carried out by the Financial Inclusion Centre has shown that almost three-quarters of people in the 18–24 and 25–39 age groups now have unsecured debts, compared with 60 percent of the 40–54 age group—showing the extent to which a new generation of debtors is emerging.[21] In 2008–10, 19 percent of people aged 16–24 were in the most indebted group of households, and 20 percent of those aged 25–34.[22] The Office for Budget Responsibility, an independent public body set up in 2010 by the government to provide impartial analysis of public finance, found in 2013 that unsecured credit growth had outpaced all other lending so far that year (the same year that the UK first started discussing the economic recovery after the recession), mostly through unsecured loans rather than credit card lending.[23] It has also been found by the debt advice charity StepChange that of the 36,413 people with payday loan debts they helped in 2012 their average income was just £1,298, whereas the average payday loan debt of those clients was £1,665.[24]

The extent to which this rise of indebtedness has coincided with a prolonged period of deteriorating incomes is demonstrated in a variety of ways. The influential think-tank The Resolution Foundation found that the economic recession had pushed 1.4m employees below the Living Wage (the rate deemed necessary for a basic standard of living), which meant in total that around 4.8m Britons (20 percent of all employees) earn below the Living Wage. Compared with 2009, the height of the recession, that figure was 3.4m (14 percent of all employees).[25] Another influential think-tank, The Joseph Rowntree Foundation, pointed out that in 2013 over half of the 13m people in poverty (surviving on less than 60 percent of the national median income) were from working families.[26] One of the major effects of the recession has been the growth of the working poor—to the extent where at the end of 2013 most of the households in poverty were in work, not out of work. This has been boosted, also, by the growth in zero-hour contract jobs,[27] "under-employment,"[28] or the significance of the lower paying sector in today's jobs market.[29]

Over the years studies have found that the usual methods of deciphering debt, and indeed dangerous debt, were not necessarily reflective of the reality of the situation. Bridges and Disney, for example, find that low-income families are not simply financially excluded; rather, these families utilize various credit arrangements. For example, in their research they find that tenants are far more likely to be in arrears on a variety of loans than homeowners; while they suggest their research topic is difficult to discern, they provide some evidence to suggest that these families minimize on borrowing costs by defaulting on family loans and by using utility nonpayments and rent arrears in the short run as a means of deferring expenditures.[30] Over 10 years later the think-tank Demos came closest to adding some meat to these findings by calling for the official measure of debt needs to be changed to include not just debt but also arrears on housing and utilities. Their research, based on the polling of over 2,000 UK adults, found that 1 in 10 people had got into debt to pay their rent.[31]

The Demos research also provides focus on the growth of the UK payday lending industry. Intriguingly, while only 6 percent of people responding to the researcher's survey had ever used a payday loan, the report found, based upon their Harm Index which combines the financial, emotional, and social consequences of taking on a particular credit product, that payday lending is the most harmful type of debt, with the exception of illegal loans, that an individual can obtain. This illustrates why, despite the fact the industry is relatively less lucrative than other industries providing consumer credit, it receives disproportionately more press attention. One respected financial commentator in 2011 raised the question of whether payday lending is really wrong, by referring to the industry's own finances compared to the volume of consumer credit in general: "Payday lending," it is pointed out, "is said by one analyst to be up from £100m in 2004 to £1.7bn in 2010. But that's modest compared with over £55bn of outstanding credit card debt or more than £200bn of consumer credit."[32] However, not only is this outsmarted by the aforementioned Demos research, but what also should be taken into consideration is the relatively small amount of time that the payday lending industry has grown in. Looked at another way, and with the benefit of newer figures, in just 10 years the payday lending industry has grown from being worth just £100m in 2004 to £2.2bn in 2014. According to the Office of Fair Trading in 2012 a total of £3.7bn worth of credit was extended by way of short-term loans by payday lenders while their borrowers paid over £900m in interest.[33] Indeed this doesn't look set to slow down any time soon: Ellison et al. in 2011 demonstrated in their research that the use of unsecured credit had declined since 2008, at the height of the recession, in all categories except high-cost credit—including from payday lenders.[34]

A renewed focus on regulation and the building up of alternative finance

In 2010 one member of the UK parliament stood out as a crusader against the payday lending industry: Stella Creasy MP. In 2010 she raised the issue of payday lending, at that time rather invisible to many politicians and the wider public alike, in a 10-minute rule bill, a way in which backbench members of parliament are able to try and introduce legislation. Creasy was aiming to introduce the Consumer Credit (Regulation and Advice) Bill 2010–12, something that would have given lawmakers the ability to cap interest rates and fee charges. For one of the first times in the UK vocabulary Creasy introduced the Total Cost of Credit cap, that is, a price ceiling on how much a lender can charge in absolute terms, including interest on the principal, fees, and other ways of introducing extra costs to a loan contract. Not surprisingly, given the policy on introducing regulations by the then new coalition government of Conservatives and Liberal Democrats (in their coalition agreement they had decided on an one-in-one-out policy regarding regulation), Creasy's bill wasn't passed. But the principle of what she called for didn't disappear either.

Over the next few years some rather alarming scandals were to hit the industry. The National Debtline, while recording just 465 calls in 2007 regarding payday lending, saw that number shoot up to 100 every day in 2013.[35] Citizens Advice, another debt advice charity, went to press regarding frequent complaints they had received including people being sold payday loans while drunk, to under-18s, and to people with mental health difficulties.[36] These stories and others set about a raised consciousness among the public on the perceived dangers of payday loans. Justin Welby, the Archbishop of Canterbury, also waded into the debate and managed to grab the attention of an international public by telling one large payday lending company, Wonga.com, an online-only payday lender who in 2012 made £1m every week in profit, that he would see to it that the Church of England compete Wonga out of business.[37] The Archbishop pledged to do this by helping grow 500 cooperative banks and credit unions, even allowing such financial institutions to operate out of the backs of churches and other community locations.

As previously mentioned, when the term financial exclusion first appeared in 1993 by academics Andrew Leyton and Nigel Thrift it had referred primarily to the limited physical access individuals had to banking services as a result of bank branch closures.[38] When the issue became more widely discussed by Karen Rowlingson and the personal finance school at Bristol it had laid less emphasis on banks, per se, and more on appropriate financial products as a means of provision.[39] Later still came a focus on affordable credit, which carried on the narrative of appropriate products. Kempson and Collard found in their research on affordable credit that the most appropriate solution for the poorest people lies in further increases to the Social Fund budget. In their words, "Moves towards larger, more professionally run credit unions and regional, community-based loan schemes, run in partnership with banks, seem particularly promising."[40] In 2013 it was decided by the government that the social fund, which was an interest-free loan that helped people in receipt of benefits meet the costs of living, would be reformed. Changes made to it meant that local authorities were in charge of its distribution, and funding for it non-ring-fenced and localized, not from the central government, meaning its allocation was subject to local government affordability in light of extensive budget cuts.[41] Rather than be rolled out further, as Kempson and Collard recommended, it was being rolled in.

Credit unions on the other hand have gained momentum in the UK, particularly since the Archbishop's announcement. Credit unions and other community development finance institutions (CDFIs) serve around 4 percent of the population. A consumer survey commissioned by the Department for Work and Pensions (DWP) demonstrated that 60 percent of low-income consumers wanted the type of product and services, including free face-to-face debt advice, that credit unions and CDFIs provide but only 13 percent were aware of the services provided.[42] From 2012 the DWP would set out plans for a £38m Credit Union Expansion Project, a three year project which will be managed by the Association of British Credit Unions Limited (ABCUL). During the DWP's analysis it was found that currently as it stands the credit union/CDFI model was unsustainable, cost structures too high, and the gap between cost and income desperately needing to be bridged. One report has suggested that even with modernization process, the best that credit unions can hope for come 2015 is a sector serving no more than 8 percent of the lower income population, or some 2m members.[43]

Previous efforts in the UK to build up the capacity for credit unions to operate among more of the low-income community, and curb the demand that high-cost credit has had in recent times, have run into similar problems. The DWP Growth Fund, spanning July 2006 up until the end of September 2010, had the objective in place to raise levels of access to affordable credit by building the capacity of third-sector lenders to serve financially excluded households. In doing so, the Growth Fund aimed to disrupt the role of high-cost credit in the lives of borrowers. The evaluation of the fund, carried out by researchers at the Personal Finance Research Centre, reported that on average 30 percent of all successful loan applicants reported having a recent record of borrowing from a high-cost lender, and 98 percent of successful loan applicants reported taking out high-cost credit at some point in their lives.[44] The extension of 317,798 Growth Fund loans from July 2006 until September 2010, and an additional 12,090 loans in October 2010, had reduced the uptake of expensive credit to those people. Sadly, however, at the same time as the Growth Fund had concluded, the payday lending industry grew substantially with an estimated £900m worth of loans extended in 2010.[45]

Another effort was taken in 2009 to emulate the best of the home credit industry, but without the price that can often end up coming attached with annualized percentage rates of hundreds of percent. After it was found that many customers of home credit claimed not to mind the cost since the benefits of the convenience (a seller comes to the house rather than the borrower going to a shop or online) research was carried out to see the extent to which a not-for-profit service could be carried out at a fraction of the typical high-cost home credit product. The result was that such a loan would still be very expensive. To break even on a home-delivered loan the interest rate would have to be around 129 percent for an average 56 week loan of £288. The model becomes cash positive by year five and assume an investment of £18m, but for the rate of a loan to be under 100 percent, to ensure it is an appropriate product for somebody on a low income, the investment would have to be £90m[46]—a long way over the current investment of £38m for the Credit Union Expansion Project.

Similar to this is a product on the market since 2012 called CUOK, a payday loan-type product, relatively short term and primarily for riskier or credit-impaired consumers, run by the London Mutual Credit Union. In the evaluation of its first year pilot it was found that applicants liked the option of repaying payday loans over a longer repayment term than usually offered from a high-cost credit lender. Just 29 percent of loan applicants wanted to borrow over the traditional one-month term, with the majority (59 percent) opting to repay over three months. It proved rather successful with 6,087 applications received (or 500 each month), requesting just under £1.5m or an average requested loan amount of £238. Researchers found that if the 7.4–8.2m payday loans estimated to have been taken out in 2011/12 from high-cost lenders had been through a credit union alternative, it is supposed that between £676m and £749m would have been saved, the equivalent of an average saving of at least £91.43 for every payday loan.[47] The CUOK loan, it should be noted, is a loss leader, that's to say that in its initial development at least it would lose money and require cross-subsidizing. It has been noted elsewhere that the average loan would require a subsidy of £6.85 to break-even. However, credit unions, the only financial institutions in the UK to have a legislated interest rate cap of 26.8 percent (in the Credit Union Act 1979), will as of April 1, 2014, be able to sell loans at 42.6 percent. It has been postulated that with this rise in interest rate the CUOK will be able to be sold at a break-even rate.[48]

The cap on the cost of payday loans

Coming back to the comments by the Archbishop of Canterbury in 2013, it ought to be pointed out that as well as wanting to compete Wonga out of the market, he also, back in 2012, gave support to the idea of a total cap on the cost of credit. Back when he was the Bishop of Durham he called payday loan companies "morally wrong" and the interest they charge a "sin."[49] He then called for the then future regulator, the Financial Conduct Authority (FCA), to cap the rate of interest and all charges that a company can charge. Eventually a cap on the cost of credit was featured in the Financial Services Act 2012, though it was not specified. It proved to be one step forward for critics of the payday industry, two steps back. Not only did researchers at the Personal Finance Research Centre publish a paper with the Department for Business, Industry and Skills (BIS) in March 2013[50] to say that there was not enough evidence that a cap on the total cost of credit would benefit consumers, and potentially even reduce their choice or leave them in the arms of illegal credit lenders, but the next month in April the Financial Conduct Authority published an Occasional Paper applying behavioral economics that said "caps on APRs or restrictions on how often [consumers] can borrow might make their financial situation worse."[51]

At what seemed like the final matter in the situation, particularly with a Conservative-led government who have historically viewed regulation in finance unfavorably, a surprise U-turn in November 2013 resulted in the Chancellor of the Exchequer George Osborne committing to setting a cap on the total cost of credit and the inclusion of a cap in the Banking Reform Bill.[52] This had all started when Lord Sharkey, a member of the House of Lords, submitted an amendment into the Banking Reform Bill which would require the FCA to implement a regulatory system like that of Florida which has a 10 percent cap on the cost of credit.[53] Interestingly, however, the cap will only apply to payday lenders and not other forms of consumer credit, which inevitably means it will miss predatory lending practices and prices elsewhere. It also incentivizes payday lenders to redefine their credit product.[54] As yet there has been no firm commitment on what the cap on the total cost of credit will look like.

Additions to the regulatory architecture in the UK, which other researchers have recommended, include a real-time database that the regulator can be in charge of and have access to that records credit transactions and ensures against borrower debt cycles,[55] better standards regarding advertising by payday lenders, and a more prescriptive rulebook on what constitutes good practice with financial warnings on websites with information on where to seek debt advice,[56] a "polluter pays" model that would see the payday lending industry pay more toward a levy on credit lenders according to the harm its loans cause,[57] and a one-off levy of £450m on the whole consumer credit industry that would then be used to create enough affordable lenders to outdo the high-cost credit industry.[58] While the UK has had a long-term understanding of financial inclusion and exclusion, attempts to temper the high-cost credit industry have largely failed. The inability of banks to lend to low-income communities, either because of the capital adequacy requirements stipulated in the Third Basel Accord[59] or because of a certain type of reputation and image that banks would prefer to cultivate,[60] the low memberships of credit unions, and the rise of people struggling to get to the end of the month without borrowing have meant that the UK has one of Europe's largest volume of outstanding unsecured loans. The response to payday lending has historically been lackluster, too: from denial by the DTI to indecision the UK has a lot to learn from abroad.

Notes

1 O'Connell, Sean (2009), *Credit and Community: Working-Class Debt in the UK since 1880*, Oxford: Oxford University Press.
2 Walker, Peter, US payday loan firms plan rapid expansion in cash-strapped Britain, *Guardian*, February 11, 2011. Available here: http://www.theguardian.com/money/2011/feb/11/us-payday-loan-firms-expansion
3 O'Connor, Sarah, Payday sector in search of new frontier, *Financial Times*, December 6, 2011. Available here: http://www.ft.com/cms/s/0/e52da39e-2011-11e1-8462-00144feabdc0.html#axzz32FfogdAK
4 Devenney, James, and Kenny, Mel (eds) (2012), *Consumer Credit, Debt and Investment in Europe*, UK: Cambridge University Press.
5 Fearon, Peter, Women Moneylenders in Liverpool: 1920s to 1940s (Draft Paper). Available here: www.ehs.org.uk/dotAsset/ec6bf4df-4482-4746-b269-f842e4c1284c.doc
6 Goode, R. M. (1979), *Consumer Credit Act: A Students Guide*, UK: Butterworth.

7   Gibbons, Damon (2014), *Britain's Personal Debt Crisis*, UK: Searching Finance.
8   Bizley, MTL (1966), The rate of interest under the Moneylenders Act, 1927, *Journal of the Institute of Actuaries*, Vol. 92: 340–346.
9   Consumer Credit: The Crowther Report (1972), *Hansard*. Available here: http://hansard.millbanksystems.com/lords/1972/jun/28/consumer-credit-the-crowther-report
10   Fernandez-Corugedo, Emilio and Muellbauer, John (2006), *Consumer Credit Conditions in the United Kingdom*, UK: Bank of England Working Paper, No. 314.
11   While there has been much academic discussion over this point, it is worth noting that Nigel Lawson, the UK's Chancellor of the Exchequer at the time of the "Big Bang" economic policy, said in 2010 that the 2007–2012 global financial crisis was an "unintended consequence" of the "Big Bang."
12   HM Treasury (2007), *Financial Inclusion: the Way Forward*, London: HM Treasury.
13   Kempson, Elaine and Collard, Sharon (2012), *Developing a Vision for Financial Inclusion*, London: Friends Provident Foundation.
14   See, for example, iff/ZEW (2010), Study on interest rate restrictions in the EU, Final Report for the EU Commission DG Internal Market and Services, Brussels/Hamburg/Mannheim: Institut für Finanzdienstleistungen.
15   Reifner, Prof. Udo (2004), DTI Study: "The effect of interest rate controls in other countries" (Germany, France and US): Preliminary Remarks from a German Perspective, Hamburg: Institut für Finanzdienstleistungen.
16   Leyshon, Andrew, and Thrift, Nigel (1995), Geographies of financial exclusion: financial abandonment in Britain and the United States, *Transactions of the Institute of British Geographers*, London: New Series.
17   Kempson, Elaine and Whyley, Claire (1998), *Access to Current Accounts*, London: British Bankers Association; Kempson, Elaine (1998), *Savings and Low Income and Ethnic Minority Households*, London: Personal Investment Authority; Rowlingson, Karen et al. (1999), *Wealth in Britain—A Lifecycle Perspective*, London: Policy Studies Institute.
18   European Commission (2008), *Financial Services Provision and Prevention of Financial Exclusion*, Brussels: Directorate-General for Employment, Social Affairs and Equal Opportunities; Department for Work and Pensions (2012), *Family Resources Survey, Stages of Producing the 2009/10 Survey's Publications*, London: Department of Work and Pensions; Kempson, Elaine and Collard, Sharon (2012), *Developing a Vision for Financial Inclusion*, London: Friends Provident Foundation.
19   Rowlingson, Karen, and McKay, Stephen (2013), *Financial Inclusion Annual Monitoring Report 2013*, Birmingham: University of Birmingham.
20   Centre for Social Justice (2013), *Maxed Out: Serious Personal Debt in Britain*, London: Centre for Social Justice.

52   Payday Lending

21 The Financial Inclusion Centre (2011), *Debt and the Family Series: Report 2: Debt and the Generations*, London: The Financial Inclusion Centre.
22 Office of National Statistics (2012), *Wealth in Great Britain Wave 2, 2008–2010 (Part 2)*, London: Office of National Statistics.
23 Office for Budget Responsibility (2013), *Economic and Fiscal Outlook—December 2013*, London: Office for Budget Responsibility.
24 StepChange, Further action needed on payday loans, *StepChange*, July 30, 2013.
25 Whittaker, Matthew, and Hurrell, Alex (2013), *Low Pay Britain 2013*, London: The Resolution Foundation.
26 MacInnes, Tom et al. (2013), *Monitoring Poverty and Social Exclusion 2013*, London: The Joseph Rowntree Foundation.
27 BBC News, What are zero-hours contracts?, *BBC News*, April 30, 2014. Available here: http://www.bbc.co.uk/news/business-23573442
28 The Huffington Post UK, UK Unemployment: Record Underemployment As 1.46m Brits Working Part-Time, *Huffington Post UK*, November 13, 2013. Available here: http://www.huffingtonpost.co.uk/2013/11/13/uk-employment-figures_n_4265134.html
29 Trades Union Congress, Four in five jobs created since June 2010 have been in low-paid industries, *TUC*, July 12, 2013. Available here: http://www.tuc.org.uk/economic-issues/labour-market/four-five-jobs-created-june-2010-have-been-low-paid-industries
30 Bridges, Sarah, and Disney, Richard (2004), *Use of Credit and Arrears on Debt Among Low-income Families in the United Kingdom*, London: Institute for Fiscal Studies.
31 Salter, Jo (2014), *The Borrowers*, London: Demos.
32 Harford, Tim, Is payday lending really wrong? *Financial Times*, December 9, 2011. Available here: http://www.ft.com/cms/s/0/3cc4eab4-21ab-11e1-a1d8-00144feabdc0.html#axzz32qcEZ3Ax. Also the value of the consumer credit industry in the UK has elsewhere been put at £180bn. See Lawrence, Mathew and Cooke, Graeme (2014), *Jumping the Shark: Building Institutions to Spread Access to Affordable Credit*, London: IPPR.
33 Office of Fair Trading (2013), *Evaluating the Impact of the 2008 OFT Market Study and UTCCR Test Case into Personal Current Accounts*, London: Office of Fair Trading.
34 Ellison, A. et al. (2011), *Credit and Low-income Consumers: A Demand-side Perspective on the Issues for Consumer Protection*, UK: Friends Provident Foundation.
35 Osborne, Hilary, Payday loans cause huge rise in calls to National Debtline, *Guardian*, February 27, 2013. Available here: http://www.theguardian.com/money/2013/feb/27/payday-loans-calls-debtline
36 Poulter, Sean, Payday loan firms 'are out of control': They exploit the mentally ill, under-18s and even drunks, finds damning report by Citizens

Advice, *Daily Mail*, May 28, 2013. Available here: http://www.dailymail.co.uk/news/article-2331895/Payday-loan-firms-control-exploit-mentally-ill-says-Citizens-Advice-report.html

37 Macrory, Sam, Archbishop's Move: Can Welby restore faith in the church?, *Total Politics*, July 24, 2013. Available here: http://www.totalpolitics.com/articles/384457/archbishopand39s-move-can-welby-restore-faith-in-the-church.thtml

38 Leyshon, Andrew, and Thrift, Nigel (1995), Geographies of financial exclusion: financial abandonment in Britain and the United States (1995), *Transactions of the Institute of British Geographers*, London: New Series.

39 Rowlingson, Karen et al. (1999), *Wealth in Britain—A Lifecycle Perspective*, London: Policy Studies Institute.

40 Kempson, Elaine, and Collard, Sharon (2005), *Affordable Credit. The Way Forward*, London: Joseph Rowntree Foundation.

41 For more information see: Packman, Carl, Amid the fury, the closure of the social fund is a quiet tragedy, *New Statesman*, April 3, 2013. Available here: http://www.newstatesman.com/business/2013/04/amid-fury-closure-social-fund-quiet-tragedy

42 DWP (2011), *Credit Union Expansion Project: Feasibility Study Report*, London: Department for Work and Pensions.

43 Henry, Dr Nick and Craig, Philip (2013), *Mind the Gap: Evidencing Demand for Community Finance*, London: Community Development Finance Association.

44 Collard, Sharon et al. (2010), *Evaluation of the DWP Growth Fund*, Bristol: Personal Finance Research Centre, University of Bristol.

45 Office of Fair Trading (2009), Review of high-cost credit: interim research report, London: Office of Fair Trading. A wider discussion of the growth in payday lending around this period can be found in Gibbons, Damon et al. (2010), *Payday Lending in the UK: A Review of the Debate and Policy Options*, London: Centre for Responsible Credit.

46 Kempson, Elaine et al. (2009), *Is a Not-For-Profit Home Credit Business Feasible?*, London: Joseph Rowntree Foundation.

47 Evans, Gareth and McAteer, Mick (2013), *Can Payday Loan Alternatives be Affordable and Viable? An Evaluation of London Mutual Credit Union's Pilot Scheme*, London: Financial Inclusion Centre.

48 Gibbons, Damon (2013), *Tackling the High Cost Credit Problem: The Importance of Real-Time Regulatory Databases*, London: Centre for Responsible Credit.

49 Mendick, Robert, Justin Welby, the Bishop of Durham, calls for cap on total cost of payday loans, *Daily Telegraph*, November 25, 2012. Available here: http://www.telegraph.co.uk/news/religion/9700796/Justin-Welby-the-Bishop-of-Durham-calls-for-cap-on-total-cost-of-payday-loans.html

50 Department for Business, Innovation and Skills (2013), *The Impact on Business and Consumers of a Cap on the Total Cost of Credit*, London: Personal Finance Research Centre.
51 Erta, Kristine et al. (2013), *Applying Behavioural Economics at the Financial Conduct Authority*, London: Financial Conduct Authority.
52 Some believe the decision to turn back on previous principles was due to a realization that capping the costs of payday lending was becoming rather popular.
53 There is a very interesting discussion on this development in Gibbons, Damon (2014), *Britain's Personal Debt Crisis*, UK: Searching Finance.
54 There has been, for example, a rise in installment lending in Australia after efforts to tackle the predatory lending practices in the payday lending industry.
55 Gibbons, Damon (2013), *Tackling the High Cost Credit Problem: The Importance of Real-time Regulatory Databases*, London: Centre for Responsible Credit.
56 Movement for Change, Sharkstoppers target payday loan advertising and payroll schemes, *Movement for Change*. Date unavailable. Available here: http://www.movementforchange.org.uk/sharkstoppers_target_payday_loan_advertising_and_payroll_schemes
57 Salter, Jo (2014), *The Borrowers*, London: Demos.
58 Lawrence, Mathew and Cooke, Graeme (2014), *Jumping the Shark: Building Institutions to Spread Access to Affordable Credit*, London: IPPR.
59 Sharifi, Shahram, and Flores, Michael G. (2013), *Options for Short-Term Credit in the United Kingdom*. Online: Social Science Research Network (SSRN). Available here: http://ssrn.com/abstract=2259542.
60 Bates, Richard et al. (2010), *Opportunity Knocks Providing Alternative Banking Solutions for Low-Income Consumers at the Post Office*, London: Consumer Focus.

3
The European Directive to Consume

Abstract: *The chapter on Europe looks at the European laws regulating consumer credit and the notion of overindebtedness that raised public consciousness around the effects of debt, and addresses the existence of high-cost credit across the union member states. It looks at the part that usury laws have played in resistance to payday lending, specific countries that have had a high presence of predatory companies, specific measures as well as European-wide measures to deal with overindebted populations, and finally the supply of alternative finance.*

Keywords: credit; debt; Europe; European Union; overindebtedness

Packman, Carl. *Payday Lending: Global Growth of the High-Cost Credit Market.* New York: Palgrave MacMillan, 2014. DOI: 10.1057/9781137361103.0006.

The European Union is the partnership of 28 countries bringing together both political and economic unity. The historical lineage of the union stems from post-World War II. After the end of the war it was to be ensured by Europeans, on seeing the destruction that had been left behind, that no war of European countries should happen again. What eventually resulted was the European Economic Community (EEC) created in 1958 with six member countries: Belgium, Germany, France, Italy, Luxembourg, and the Netherlands. In 1993, the name was changed to the European Union to reflect the change in remit from economic community to a union based on shared political values. On 1 November of that year the Maastricht Treaty had been established, signed the year before by members of the European Communities and has since been amended by the treaties of Amsterdam, Nice, and Lisbon, the latter coming into force in 2009. The monetary union was established in 1999, at which point exchange rates were frozen and fixed, but came into full force (both electronic money and coinage) in 2002, composed as it stands of 18 member states that use the euro as their legal tender.

From the second half of the 1980s onward the European Commission (EC) adopted a number of directives that principally aimed to protect consumers in a contractual setting, the first being the Doorstep Selling Directive of 1985, followed by the Consumer Credit Directive in 1987. There was to be "minimal harmonization" of laws at this stage, resulting in the member countries adopting their own standards regarding the consumer. In 1997 the Distance Selling Directive, which had been concerned with credit transactions that take place away from a business premises, such as doorstep lending from home credit operators, was eventually adopted in the Distance Selling Directive for Financial Services in 2002.[1] It has been commented that the focus on consumer protection was in order that at the end of a credit transaction the result is not overwhelming for the consumer, especially given the growing overindebtedness of private households.[2]

Certainly there was a precedent to set. It hasn't gone unnoticed by governments across Europe that left to their own devices the unscrupulous portion of big business and the financial industry will try and deceive consumers. One of the guiding principles of legislation and statecraft within a market system is to anticipate, in a proportionate manner, the way in which the unscrupulous may try to deceive. While this may be par for the course of a democratic system, in a European context it also closely connected to usury. Professor Udo Reifner, looking at usury law in the context of the European Union, noted that in Catholic culture, high interest tends to be identified with exploitation while in Protestant cultures on the other hand it reflects high risk.[3] While this has not been the primary approach by researchers looking at the status of the consumer within a unified Europe, the extent to which the overtly religious topic of usury plays out in a system that has, for the most part, unified countries who have both Catholicism and Protestantism as key parts of their historical and cultural identities cannot go unnoticed. It is no surprise, of course, to find that many European countries have usury explicitly written into their criminal and civil codes, more on which toward the middle of this chapter.

Greater harmonization of European laws in the early 1990s took place in the context of liberalized markets.[4] The Consumer Credit Directive, as it was changed in both 2008 and 2010, has been the subject of some debate as to whether it moved with the times to be more on the side of lenders and creditors, not borrowers (as is the general critique of increased financialization), or desperately trying to act as a corrective to a growing part of the population becoming wedded to debt and overindebtedness. Certainly as regards information and the "informed consumer" things improved under the Consumer Credit Directive 2008. In relation to costs and the Annual Percentage Rate of charge, recital 19 pointed out that: "In order to enable consumers to make their decisions in full knowledge of the facts, they should receive adequate information... prior to the conclusion of the credit agreement." APR, it was also noted, would be determined in the same way throughout the European Community.

While building up the capacity of the informed consumer was all well and good, the debt-burdened household was already looming large over the heads of European regulators and policymakers. As like the United States and elsewhere the majority of the population was not in hock to financial institutions, however it was less about the volume of people in debt, rather, the severity of those debts. Moreover, the Europe 2020 strategy, written in 2010, setting out an objective of the European Union to life at the very least 20m people out of poverty was looking like a distant pipe dream, not least because of the financial crisis. As a response the European Commission, the executive body of the European Union responsible for legislation, carried out a study aimed at developing a common definition of overindebtedness across the whole of the EU.[5] This in turn raised the consciousness about debt on a Europe-wide level and, indeed, the consumer credit industries of each member country.

The role of overindebtedness in raising consciousness of the consumer credit industry

It is really no surprise that overindebtedness should take the European Commission's focus given that leading up to it in the early and mid-2000s it received a good deal of attention from academics looking at Europe. The focus, in the main, for researchers on overindebtedness has been its proximity to the problem of the unbanked (and how at first that may seem counterintuitive), its relation to purchasing power, the impact of neoliberalism, and the issue of insolvency.[6] To quantify the problem, it was found that many EU citizens were struggling to service their mortgages or consumer credit, and to pay their rent and utility bills. In 2010, more than one in four individuals reported that they felt at risk of becoming overindebted, while 11.6 percent were in arrears with payments related to such debts or bills (up from 9.9 percent in 2007). Two years earlier it was found that one out of every five households in the EU reported a major drop in income over the previous year, mainly related to job losses.[7] Most worryingly for the so-called Generation Debt[8] is that when asked in 2010 around 27 percent of EU27 residents aged 15 years and older reported feeling "very" or "fairly" at risk of being overindebted.[9] The proportion of EU residents who felt at risk of being overindebted stayed at a constant in 2009–10; however, in 2010 some 11.6 percent of EU residents reported to being in arrears of payments related to debts or bills over the previous 12 months, up from 9.9 percent in 2007.[10]

While this might explain the outlook, from a policy focus it cannot, by itself, explain what went wrong. Others addressing the topic of overindebtedness have, however, attempted to do so. Huls et al pointed out that too few measures were in place at a policy level to protect consumers from "undue demands and harassment," beating many other analysts in anticipating an irreversible move away from a purely consumer-focused environment in the 1980s to one geared closer to lender focused[11]; the fair and equitable allocation of consumer credit, and the risks associated with this, should be shared by both consumers and lenders alike to allow the former, in difficult times, to a "reasonable standard of living"[12]; an opportunity for a "fresh start" should be written and enforced in law in order to reflect "the European moral attitude toward payment of debts," as well as free budget and debt counseling available to consumers[13]; and *measures* to prevent excessive consumer credit alongside measures to facilitate rehabilitation which may include: encouraging effective financial inclusion, a realistic view of debtor obligations paying only as much as possible, and fostering payment plans that do not "deprive the debtor and/or his family of the ability to satisfy their basic needs with due regard to their human dignity."[14]

Understandably, given the precarious position into which many consumers had found themselves, the focus with this research angle was that it was geared on crisis management. The real ingenuity on this came from individual member states who devised insolvency policies that could be then taken as best practice around the union. Individual debtors with large debt burdens were largely ignored by European insolvency laws until the late twentieth century and even then in sporadic way across European Union member states.[15] However, what in the meantime was needed was a program for responsible credit at the point of a credit agreement.

In 2006 the European Coalition for Responsible Credit, a network of agencies aiming to influence European policy, had written a manifesto of principles for responsible credit. Professor Udo Reifner called this type of "productive" credit, the type "that neither leads to impoverishment nor to over-indebtedness."[16] The first principles of responsible and affordable credit are based on the ideal that credit is essential for full participation in society; banks should not discriminate and should provide real credit access; and, credit to consumers and small businesses must be supervised. As such, credit contracts ought to be exclusive of hidden fees or involve multiple firms that may cause the consumer involved distress; credit contracts are usually extended by private firms and as such those firms should not be left entirely to their own devices, as is the principle of the "invisible hand," which is already appreciated within Europe's existing tradition against usury[17]; and, credit contracts must not risk losing the social responsibility and "good morals" of previous consumer credit directives (related to early drafts of what came to be the EU Consumer Credit Directive 2008/48/EC which was at risk of losing commitments to improved consumer protection). In short, responsible and affordable credit for all, credit relations that are transparent and understandable, productive for the borrower, adaptation rather than credit cancellation and default charges should only be used to cover losses, protective legislation over all credit provision (bank and nonbank), effective individual and collective rights to legal procedures.[18]

Another debate develops: should those in debt not at least be glad of their relative fortune? In a study on the link between financial exclusion and overindebtedness it is found that in most European countries where overindebtedness has been studied (such as Austria, Belgium, France, Germany, Ireland, the Netherlands, Norway, and the UK), it may appear that the main triggers for overindebtedness are life changes (e.g., job loss, separation or divorce, or sickness).[19] However, rather than seeing overindebtedness simply as a particular oversight of policymakers, some researchers, looking at European consumer credit policy through the lens of neoliberalism,[20] financialization,[21] and from within the "competitive social market economy," have raised questions about the longer term trend: Was the growing personal debt of European citizens not the expected outcome of a European policy committed to competition among lenders, not the welfare of borrowers? That debate continues, however yet another question arises: What part has financial exclusion and overindebtedness played in the existence of high-cost credit in Europe?

The supply of high-cost credit within the European Union

To begin with there are difficulties. While it is necessary when making an evaluation and judgment upon the influence of the high-cost credit industry within a country or union of countries to look at the stock of personal debt that exists within it, unfortunately for research purposes alone it is not possible to do this in reverse, that is to say look at debt and expect to get an idea of the part high-cost credit plays in that. That is where we are in much of Europe. While we can even trace which companies operate where,[22] this still gives us limited appreciation of its penetration. Given the lack of information and access to the finances of larger payday loans firms, hidden on the grounds of commercial sensitivity, it is not possible to find individual breakdowns which would provide us with the necessary details to see how much of an individual country's consumer credit market is occupied by them. With limited previous research on the extent to which payday lending, for example, has taken off in Europe (with the exception of some noted countries), or indeed how it differs from the way it operates in more established places such as Australia or the United States, for what there is can raise more questions than it answers. For example, while one piece of research looking at consumer credit mentions that Ireland has a rapidly developing payday loans sector, another report focusing on the issue says that the Central Bank and the Regulators in Ireland have done very well to keep payday loans to a minimum.[23]

The other way to see this, however, is that the high-cost credit industry simply hasn't the same sway in most parts of Europe, and there is very good reason to suspect this is the case. Research by Beddows and McAteer, looking into the practices of the payday lending more generally, attempted to gain a sense of how much revenue is made by one of the largest global providers of online payday loans, Dollar Financial, by looking at their Earnings Call. In so doing it is found that by a long way the company's UK online lending raises the most revenue, according to interview material with a Dollar Financial executive, but no precise figure on how much is then raised in Scandinavia, Eastern Europe, and Canada where the company also operates.

In trying to find an answer to the Europe question it is also necessary to consider if the concept of "usury," "extortionate pricing," and "unfair credit" has significant legal clout. The word usury, for example, in Italy, Malta, Estonia, Denmark may be used indirectly in the context of criminal lending, but in countries such as Portugal, France, Belgium, Spain, Slovenia, the Czech Republic, Slovakia, Hungary, Ireland, the UK, and Germany it can mean high-priced loans more broadly. Most importantly however, usury exists as a legal concept in the criminal and/or the civil codes of 21 Member States. Denmark, Finland, Latvia, Romania, Slovenia, and Malta, for example, have incorporated usury within their criminal codes. Estonia, France, Hungary, Bulgaria, and Spain have incorporated usury within their civil codes, and Czech Republic, Belgium, Austria, Germany, Greece, Portugal, Slovakia, Poland, Sweden, and Italy have incorporated usury within both their criminal and civil codes.[24]

It should be remembered that many countries have strict interest rate caps in Europe. It is interesting to note, for example, the different reasons that are given for why a country has developed a fixed interest rate restriction. In Belgium for example, it is primarily to prevent excessive rates by lenders, while in Estonia it was in order to control overindebtedness. In the Netherlands it was used as a way of controlling illegal financial activities and protecting consumers by preventing the charging of excessive interest rates and decreasing risk-taking behavior on the part of credit providers, and in Poland it was to protect borrowers from excessive interest charges. While these interest rates will have a very large effect on the ability for the high-cost credit industry to make financial gains in those countries, it hasn't made it impossible. We know for example in Spain, where nearly 90 percent of the population are banked, that is to by some measures financially *included*, there is still room in the market for companies like Wonga, who in 2013 bought an online payday lender in Spain called Credito Pocket, and Kreditech, a company operating out of Munich and into places like Russia, the Czech Republic, and Mexico, that makes credit assessments on borrowers using social media sites like Facebook, and a competitor of Wonga's.

Interestingly Wonga also operates in Poland, where usury has been incorporated both into the criminal and civic codes, but, according to one report from the Bank of Spain, has a relatively lower grade of sophistication in their financial system. It may well explain why Wonga can charge 15 percent APR for a loan of 500zł ($164.64), but 80zł in commission,[25] meaning the representative APR is 585 percent, which is near the average for a payday loan in the United States.[26]

Another example, this time where it has been found that the payday lending industry has been most successful, second only to the UK, is the Netherlands. The country saw a rise in Flitskrediet ("flash credits"), which are payday loans, previously unregulated and likely to have annualized percentage rates as high as 600 percent. Flitskrediet were estimated to have around 25,000 contracts and be worth 6m euro, amounting to around 0.025 percent of the Dutch consumer credit market. What does this tell us? Namely that it doesn't occupy a lot of the consumer credit market, but that it is not necessarily a marker of whether this type of easy credit is a problem or not. What might be more telling is that the many flash credits don't break even, which is interesting given that one of the advantages for online lenders is lower operating costs, though often companies experience higher losses. The whole context around this type of product is inconclusive. Commenting on this form of product, Professor Reifner supposed that when the EU CCD 2008 comes into effect it will lead to its demise. He was later proved correct.

In 2009 The Dutch Socialist Party called for Flitskrediet to be forbidden. They asked the Minister of Finance Wouter Bos to look into the practice and associated high rates of interest. As is typical the loans were for small amounts and were to be paid back in less than three months. However, given the size of the loans they were found not covered by the regulations including the Authority for the Financial Markets (AFM) and the Act on Financial Supervision. Like in the case of Poland with Wonga while the interest rate limit was 15 percent a lender could sidestep it by charging handling fees on top of it.[27] Since 2012 there has been a series of court actions taken against short-term lenders online by the Authority for the Financial Markets (AFM). The reason being that the Act on Financial Supervision was amended due to the implementation of the Consumer Credit Directive (2008/48/EC) in May 2011.[28] In 2013 it also imposed an administrative fine on BA Finance, who trade under the name Cash Bob, and its two directors. The fines are for offering short-term loans without having obtained the correct license to do so.[29] Then again in 2014 another company, betaaldag.nl (payday.nl), was fined 2m euro after it was found that the British company was making loans outside of the rate restrictions.[30] There is a very real sense that the country once considered a target by high-cost credit lenders is taking considerable steps to control the practices of payday lending where they are deemed unfit.

Looking again more generally, to back up the thesis that payday lending has simply not had the same amount of penetration in a lot of Europe as elsewhere, where the high cost of credit in Europe has been recorded, it is more typically associated with revolving credit, which can very often be from an overdraft facility on a credit card. Indeed in Professor Reifner's study of interest rate restrictions six countries, including France and Germany, have reports of high-cost revolving credit. This ties in neatly with the encouragement by the European Commission that individuals engage with the banking system such as in France where since 1978 it has been compulsory to pay social benefit into a bank account. Though there are still differing degrees of financial exclusion,[31] the ability to get a basic bank account has been made easier by virtue of the European Commission's policy regarding basic banking services as essential services, affirming that Member States remain free to extend existing universal financial service obligations, insofar as they comply with EU law. So while many households won't be recorded as financially excluded, they might find themselves credit-impaired, or indeed have similar problems to those consumers in more relaxed financial markets in hock to payday lenders.[32]

What does this tell us? The element of conflict (or perhaps compromise) within the EU is understandable given that it is a union of countries each with its own character, often trying and struggling to pull along together. This no more perhaps than the United States, but of course the context is a lot different. Looking quite broadly at the direction of the European Commission and the individual member states the impression is, of course rather generally, that the states provided a corrective to some of the excesses, and nowhere is this more pronounced than on the matter of debt and personal finance. Consider, for example, the historical context of usury that is raised by Professor Udo Reifner against the increased financialization of the European Union; consider, also, the rise of the overindebted citizen and the attempts by individual states to pursue appropriate measures toward insolvency as an orderly resolution of personal debt overhang. In many ways the EU drags one way while those individual states seek to go another.

But what of the existence of high-cost credit? Whether it is a surprise or not to find there has been slim influence of high-cost credit depends on what one expects to see leading up to its expansion. Sure, like the United States or Australia much of the European Union is set within the context of deregulation in the 1980s and the 1990s, and with further moves toward neoliberalism, the effects of which are most certainly more marked in some places than others (the most obvious example being of course Greece). As the latter system has matured, so too has the number of working poor people. Their part in what Maurizio Lazzarato calls the flexibility of precarious full employment is writ large. Maurizio Lazzarato points out about the French Renenu de solidarité active, the welfare system, that we have passed through the old dualism of unemployment/employment to the extent where they are combined in the "poor worker," where the unemployed may have to work for nothing to claim their social security, and causally employed on zero-hours contracts may be in receipt of in-work social security because of the postindustrial rise of the low-paid job with few opportunities to progress because of the increase in robot labor; none of these things are dystopian nightmares alone anymore, they are real. And are these same people, who are growing in number across Europe and beyond, not the very same asset-limited, income-constrained, employed individuals who payday lenders have no qualms admitting are their target audience elsewhere? And don't these same lenders have a presence in European countries? Then why is there such a major difference between the United Kingdom, which as we have seen is inundated with debt and for that matter payday lending in Europe? It seems likely that when the rest of Europe kept their existing usury laws, and subsequently their interest rate restrictions, which the United Kingdom lacked, this acted as a barrier to entry for a fringe financial system that "served," and if other situations internationally are any judge, added to the debts of low-income households or the already overindebted population.

One suggestion might be that whereas the UK had grown to be rather relaxed in the 1990s and the 2000s of the small gains by fringe financiers, that in turn emerged as large gains looking at the environment now, many European countries were not. Another answer may be found in the relatively low base of the debt economy. One study by Harvard academic Gunnar Trumbull,[33] for example, notes that in 1955, nonmortgage consumer debt averaged 15 percent of household disposable income in the United States, compared to 0.3 percent in France. Fast-forward fifty years in 2005 and US nonmortgage household debt had risen to 33 percent of disposable income while French household debt was still below 15 percent of disposable income. The French in this instance have had debt-to-income ratios historically lower than America, to which Trumbull puts down to a different historical attitude to the welfare state. While, as noticed by Lazzarato above, the two countries have somewhat converged of late, as is largely the case in the globalized world, perhaps this provides another explanation as to why fringe lenders have not gained as much traction. To be sure, the movement toward the "cradle-to-grave" coverage that many European countries enjoyed after WWII, and the universal welfare model in Scandinavia[34] distinct to the partial "safety net" model, as opposed to the US "consumer republic,"[35] cannot be ignored here.

As we have seen, also, that where there has been an increased effort to enforce the wording of the Consumer Credit Directive then the penetration of short-term lenders is halted. This, alongside the interest rate restrictions, could mean that (1) fringe finance, which has often and quite rightly been reported to have a negative reputation, is dissuaded from entering the market; and/or (2) the enforcement of the CCD has been somewhat neglected in regard to mainstream banking, meaning thus that high-cost credit for consumers who pose a risk are covered by banks.[36] The last point raises a very important point: In the previous assessment of overindebtedness while it may be the case that those more likely to experience this are simultaneously experiencing life changes (job losses, changes to income) these are also the same individuals who are least able to suffer financial shocks without assistance. While it is positive that coverage of mainstream banking has for a large part of Europe meant that fringe finance and high-cost credit has not been an option, since we know from research conducted internationally that the industry tends to be predicated on a business model designed to trap rather than assist people away from debt, we cannot ignore the extent to which revolving credit, for example, or personal loans from banks that may still be expensive and contrary to the stipulated price and interest rules of the CCD, are high cost and inappropriate for some consumers. It may also explain why there has been some demand for online or SMS lenders like Wonga and Kreditech, who *can* offer something quick[37] and small sum. Though it is apparent that in the long term what people who experience financial shocks or a credit product that isn't necessarily served by mainstream banks is not an expensive short-term loan, but something more fitting that can facilitate borrowing while being responsible, and can encourage saving as well as offering face–face debt advice.

The supply of alternative finance

Europe is the home of the Credit Union. More specifically that home is in Germany. In 1836 there were around 300 Savings Banks in the country. Credit cooperatives, which would eventually come to undercut informal lenders that smallholders and the landless relied on, were first introduced during the 1850s. By 1861 Hermann Schulze-Delitzsch founded over 364 Schulze-Delitzsch Credit Cooperatives with nearly 49,000 members. In 1836 there were around 300 savings banks, but by 1913 that figure had reached over 3,000. Between that small time period access to credit and savings accounts came to make history for the way in which households, particularly low-income households, did finance.[38]

Fast-forward to a day when the European Union is undertaking rigorous austerity measures and you might imagine in the smallholders of that time, previously having to take out high-cost loans informally, the European citizens of today who no longer want to do business with their banks anymore. The IMF/ECB/EU "Troika" bailout of Irish banks that redirected the losses on to Irish citizens.[39] Incidents such as the famous ex-football player Eric Cantona encouraging people to withdraw their money from banks, the Move Your Money campaign, people in Spain going ahead and withdrawing money from banks,[40] is this the way to democratize finance in the same way that Savings Banks and credit cooperatives democratized finance in Germany in the nineteenth century? And what opportunities do EU citizens have today to do something similar?

Alternative finance has different connotations in different parts of the European Union. For example, while savings banks are considered rather more mainstream in countries such as Spain and France, in the UK these are considered alternative. But in this instance it is useful to regard alternative finance as operating for a reason, either as a reaction to the lack of appropriate credit products for low-income households (which I will distinguish from alternative profit-making alternative finance, which I have hitherto regarded as the high-cost credit industry), or as a nonprofit alternative to mainstream banks in the form of a mix of savings and loans.

One study found that in Europe there are credit unions in Belarus, Estonia, Great Britain, Ireland, Latvia, Lithuania, Macedonia, Moldova, Poland, Romania, Russia, and Ukraine. The highest number of credit unions is in Ireland, which in 2012 was 498 with a membership of 3m, some 70 percent of the population, along with assets totaling $18,289m. Poland has 59 credit unions with a membership of 2.2m, 8 percent of the population, and $4,728m assets.[41]

It is not surprising that in countries with active savings banks, there are stronger regional growth rates, such as in Austria, Germany, and Spain. What this says about the make-up and distribution methods present in those countries is besides the point, what is clear from the research, though, is that the presence of these alternative sources of finance provides a number of benefits that would be sucked out by the greater presence of high-cost credit.

The presence of cooperatives has a positive impact upon GDP in most European countries, too, namely in Austria, Finland, Germany, and the Netherlands. Because of their perceived contribution to regional growth, GDP, and what they can do to encourage personal savings behavior, the Financial Services Users Group, set up by the European Commission, called for the introduction of a European Community Reinvestment Act that would mirror the CRA in the United States.[42] It was pointed out that while the principle of information disclosure would be directly comparable to the way this is carried out in the United States, the legislation for it may be appropriate at a European level in the form of a Disclosure Directive. Unlike the case in the United States, or even the local lending databases carried out in the UK by the British Bankers Association, a EU-wide Disclosure Directive should oblige the disclosure of vital lending information from all lenders, not just those from the mainstream, and in this way would reinforce a culture whereby lenders could not expect to lend in a certain community without having some of their information more transparent. As we have seen, there is market in Europe for online and SMS payday lending but not enough is known about it. Even the biggest firms in that space are not fully open about the specifics of their operations. Finding the technological means to assess lending patterns among companies that have no shop fronts is, in terms of greater scrutiny of the entire consumer credit industry, the problem of our times. But moving more broadly toward this type of transparency, as is the principle and partial success of reinvestment acts, would not only give us more needed insight into the extent to which households are being lent to, by mainstream banks, alternative finance, and fringe finance, but also give those institutions a means to assessing whether their financial products are best suited to that consumer, on the assumption that if it wasn't then they could signpost to a lending institution that was more suitable. More exposure of credit unions, for example, may also level the playing field in countries such as Romania where they are not exempt from Article 2 of the EU Directive on Capital Requirements (CRD) which impacts on the products and services they can offer their members.

Notes

1   The Council Directive *85/577/EEC* of 20 December 1985 to protect the consumer in respect of contracts negotiated away from business premises; EU Directive 97/7/EC on the Protection of Consumers in respect of Distance Contracts; and, Directive 2002/65/EC of the European Parliament and of the Council of 23 September 2002 concerning the distance marketing of consumer financial services and amending Council Directive 90/619/EEC and Directives 97/7/EC and 98/27/EC.
2   Westphal, Manfred (2008), The EU Financial Services Policy and Its Effect on Consumer Law, In Kelly-Louw, Michelle, Nehf, James P., and Rott, Peter (eds) *The Future of Consumer Credit Regulation*, UK: Ashgate Publishing.
3   Reifner, Udo and Schröder, Michael (2012), *Usury Laws: A legal and Economic Evaluation of Interest Rate Restrictions in the European Union*, UK: Books on Demand.
4   Guttermann, Robert and Plihon, Dominique (2008), *Consumer Debt and Financial Fragility*, Paris: Conseil en Éducation des Premières Nations, 2008.
5   Fondeville, N et al. (2010), *Over-Indebtedness: New Evidence from the EU-SILC Special Module*, Luxemburg: European Commission. Discussed at length in D'Allesio, Giovanni and Iezza, Stefano (2013), *Household Over-Indebtedness Definition and Measurement with Italian Data*, Italy: Bank of Italy.

The European Directive to Consume   69

6   See, for example, Gloukoviezoff, G. (2006), From Financial Exclusion to Overindebtedness: The Paradox of Difficulties for People on Low Income?, In Anderloni, Luisa, Braga, Maria Debora, Carluccio, Emanuele Maria (eds), *New Frontiers in Banking Services: Emerging Needs and Tailored Products for Untapped Markets* (2006), Berlin: Springer Verlag; Anderloni, L. (2003), *Il Social Banking in Italia. Un Fenomeno da esplorare*, Milan: Giuffré; Anderloni, L. and Carluccio, E. (2006), Access to Bank Accounts and Payment Services, In Anderloni, L., Carluccio, E. and Braga, M. (eds), *New Frontiers in Banking Services: Emerging Needs and Tailored Products for Untapped Markets*, Berlin: Springer Verlag; Carbo, S., Gardner, E. and Molyneux, P. (2005), *Financial Exclusion*, Basingstoke: Palgrave Macmillan; Devlin J. F. (2005), A Detailed Study of Financial Exclusion in the United Kingdom, *Journal of Consumer Policy*, No. 28; Gloukoviezoff, G. (2004), *De la bancarisation de masse a l'exclusion bancaire puis sociale in "Revue Française des Affaire Sociales n3-2004"*, Paris: La Documentation Francaise; Sinclair, S. (2001), *Financial Exclusion: A Introductory Survey*, Edinburgh: Heriot Watt University Centre for Research into Socially Inclusive Services.
7   Eurofound (2012), *Household Debt Advisory Services in the European Union*, Brussels: Eurofound.
8   Referring to Kamenetz, Anya (2006), *Generation Debt: How Our Future Was Sold Out for Student Loans, Bad Jobs, No Benefits, and Tax Cuts for Rich Geezers—And How to Fight Back*, US: Riverhead Trade. In it, Kamenetz details how a generation of young people entering the labour market are being dragged down by low wages, student loans, sky-high house prices, as well as the coming retirements of their baby-boomer parents.
9   Eurobarometer (2011), *Public Opinion in the European Union*, Brussels: European Commission.
10 Eurofound (2012), *Household Debt Advisory Services in the European Union*, Brussels: Eurofound.
11 Huls, N., Reifner, U., and Bourgoinie, T. (2003), *Overindebtedness of Consumers in the EC Member States: Facts and Search for Solutions, Diegem*, Brussels: Centre de Droit de la Consommation.
12 INSOL International (2001), *Consumer Debt Report*, London: International Federation of Insolvency Professionals.
13 Reifner, Kiesiläinen, Huls and Springeneer (2003), *Consumer Over-indebtedness and Consumer Law in the European Union: Final Report*, Rotterdam: Institute for Financial Services e.V., Erasmus University Rotterdam.
14 Council of Europe (2007), *Final Activity Report of the Group of Specialists for Legal Solutions to Debt Problems (CJ-S-DEBT)*, Strasbourg: Council of Europe.
15 Niem, Johanna (2009), Overindebted Households and Law: Prevention and Rehabilitation, In Niem, Ramsay and Whitford (eds), *Consumer Credit,*

70   Payday Lending

      Debt and Bankruptcy: Comparative and International Perspectives, UK: Hart Publishing.
16   Reifner, Udo (2009), A Call to Arms—Regulation of Consumer Lending, In Niem, Ramsay and Whitford (eds), *Consumer Credit, Debt and Bankruptcy: Comparative and International Perspectives*, UK: Hart Publishing.
17   Here the ECRC's principles evoke the concept of 'laesio enormis' which Kristoffel R. Grechenig described as "The right [that] would be triggered in the case of the purchase of a painting for a presumed market value of 100, where the true value (the painting is in fact from a famous artist) is 600." See Grechenig, Kristoffel R. (2006), The Economics of the Rule of Laesio Enormis (Die laesio enormis als enorme Laesion der sozialen Wohlfahrt?), *Journal fur Rechtspolitik*, No. 1.
18   The principles are available at http://www.responsible-credit.net/media.php?id=1651. A wider discussion can be found in Reifner, Udo (2009), A Call to Arms—Regulation of Consumer Lending, In Niem, Ramsay and Whitford, *Consumer Credit, Debt and Bankruptcy: Comparative and International Perspectives*, UK: Hart Publishing.
19   Gloukoviezoff, G. (2003), The link between financial exclusion and over-indebtedness [online]. Available at http://www.ecosocdoc.be/static/module/bibliographyDocument/document/001/379.pdf.
20   See, for example, Ramsay, Iain (2010), Regulation of Consumer Credit, In Howells, Kraft and Ramsay, Wilhelmsson, *Handbook of Research on International Consumer Law*, UK: Edward Elgar Pub.; Ramsay, Iain (2003), Bankruptcy in Transition: The Case of England and Wales-the Neo-Liberal Cuckoo in the European Bankruptcy Nest?, In Whitford, W., Niemi-Kiesilainen, J. and Ramsay, I. (eds), *Consumer Bankruptcy in a Global Perspective*, Oxford: Hart Publishing; ALTER-EU (2009), *A Captive Commission: The Role of the Financial Industry in Shaping EU Regulation*, UK: Alliance for Lobbying Transparency and Ethics Regulation in the European Union.
21   See, for example, Fouskas, Vassilis K. and Dimoulas, Constantine (2013), *Greece, Financialization and the EU: The Political Economy of Debt and Destruction*, US: Palgrave Macmillan; Lazzarato, Maurizio (2012), *The Making of the Indebted Man: Essay on the Neoliberal Condition*, US: MIT; Corr, C (2006), *Financial Exclusion in Ireland: An Exploratory Study and Policy Review*, Dublin: Combat Poverty Agency.
22   For example, looking at some of the biggest companies globally, Dollar Financial Group from the US operates in UK and Ireland, Wonga from the UK operates in Poland and Spain, and Cash Converters from Australia operates in France and Spain.
23   See Financial Services User Group (2012), *Ensuring Fair, Affordable and Safe Financial Products for Vulnerable Users*, Brussels: Financial Services User Group; and Leeson, Nick, Here's one thing to congratulate the Irish

regulators for…, *TheJournal.ie,* October 29, 2012. Available at http://businessetc.thejournal.ie/readme/payday-loans-nick-leeson-647713-Oct2012/.

24 Reifner, Udo, Clerc-Renaud, Sebastien, Knobloch, and Michael, R. A. (2010), *Final Report on Interest Rate Restrictions in the E,* Hamburg: Institut für Finanzdienstleistungen e.V.

25 Information taken from https://www.wonga.pl/.

26 Where the average loan from a familiar payday lender can be 580 per cent. See here: http://extras.mnginteractive.com/live/media/site525/2014/0114/20:4 0114_073756_Dallas_Survey.pdf.

27 Emerce, Aanbod flitsleningen groeit; regels nodig, Emerce, February 18, 2008. Available at http://www.emerce.nl/nieuws/aanbod-flitsleningen-groeit-regels-nodig.

28 Ropenairain, Janice, Dutch Financial Regulator Focuses on Flash Loans, *International Finance Law Review,* August 29, 2012. Available at http://www.ifl. com/Article/3081661/Dutch-financial-regulator-focuses-on-flash-loans.html.

29 4-Traders, The Netherlands Authority for the Financial Market: Three Fines for the Illegal Offering of Payday Loans, *4-Traders,* December 16, 2012. Available at www.4-traders.com/news/The-Netherlands-Authority-for-the-Financial-Market--Three-fines-for-the-illegal-offering-of-payday--17633689/.

30 *Dutch News,* Clamp-down Drives Many Payday Loan Firms Out of Business in NL, *Dutch News,* February 13, 2014. Available at http://www.dutchnews. nl/news/archives/2014/02/clamp-down_drives_many_payday.php#sthash. W1eFYhlv.dpuf.

31 Discussed in detail in Corr, C (2006), *Financial Exclusion in Ireland: An Exploratory Study and Policy Review,* Dublin: Combat Poverty Agency.

32 Though we should remember that research in the UK for example shows that some individuals who have taken out a payday loan or loans have previously had trouble with credit cards in the past. See for example Uren, Adam, 'I was shocked they kept saying yes': Woman allowed to take out EIGHT payday loans at same time to run up £3,000 debt, This is Money, March 6, 2014. Available at: http://www.thisismoney.co.uk/money/cardsloans/article-2573686/Woman-allowed-EIGHT-payday-loans-time.html and Gentleman, Amelia, Wonga: the real cost of a payday loan, The Guardian, March 1, 2012. Available at: http://www.theguardian.com/business/2012/mar/01/wonga-real-cost-payday-loan

33 Trumbull, Gunnar (2012), Credit Access and Social Welfare The Rise of Consumer Lending in the United States and France, *Politics and Society,* Vol. 40, No. 1.

34 See Wilkinson, Richard and Pickett, Kate (2010), *The Spirit Level: Why Equality is Better for Everyone,* UK: Penguin; Kuhnle, Stein, and Hort, Sven E. O. (2004), *The Developmental Welfare State in Scandinavia: Lessons for the Developing World,* Geneva: United Nations Research Institute for Social Development.

35 Cohen, Lizabeth (2003), *A Consumers' Republic: The Politics of Mass Consumption in Postwar America*, US: Vintage Books.
36 It may suggest there has been an increase in illegal lending, too. There will be more on that subject in forthcoming chapters, but it should be noted that in Professor Udo Reifner's research this was not found to be a phenomena naturally the outcome of interest rate restrictions. Furthermore, research looking at consumer credit in the UK, France, and Germany found more instances of illegal lending in the UK, despite having no operable interest rate ceiling. See Thiel, Veronika (2009), *Doorstep Robbery: Why the UK Needs a Fair Lending Law*, UK: New Economics Foundation.
37 A price is paid for 'quick' online loans, of course. See, for details, Packman, Carl, Wonga are blinding critics with science, *New Statesman*, December 18, 2012. Available at http://www.newstatesman.com/politics/2012/12/wonga-are-blinding-critics-science; Deville, Joe, Leaky data: How Wonga makes lending decisions, Charisma Network, May 20, 2013. Available at http://www.charisma-network.net/finance/leaky-data-how-wonga-makes-lending-decisions; Evans, Tara, Wonga raids 15-year-old's bank account to recover debts after it wrongly granted fraudsters a loan with his details, *This is Money*, May 1, 2013. Available at http://www.thisismoney.co.uk/money/cardsloans/article-2317239/Wonga-raids-15-year-olds-bank-account-recover-debts-BBC-Watchdog.html; Pridmore, Jason (2012), Consumer Surveillance: Context, Perspectives and Concerns in the Personal Information Economy, In Ball, Kirstie., Haggerty, Kevin D., and Lyon, David (eds), *The Routledge Handbook of Surveillance Studies*, US: Routledge.
38 Guinnane, Timothy W. (2001), Cooperatives as Information Machines: German Rural Credit Cooperatives, 1883–1914, *The Journal of Economic History*, Vol. 61, No. 2; Simpson, C.V.J. (2013), *The German Sparkassen (Savings Banks): A Commentary and Case Study*, UK: Civitas.
39 Stamp, Stuart (2013), *Socialising the Loss, Personalising the Responsibility, and Privatising the Response: The Irish Policy Approach to Personal Debt Post 2008*, UK: Centre on Household Assets and Savings Management.
40 Willsher, Kim, Eric Cantona's call for bank protest sparks online campaign, *Guardian*, November 21, 2010. Available at http://www.theguardian.com/world/2010/nov/20/eric-cantona-bank-protest-campaign; Move Your Money campaign. See here: http://moveyourmoney.org.uk/; Lazzarato, Maurizio (2012), *The Making of the Indebted Man: Essay on the Neoliberal Condition*, US: MIT.
41 Financial Services User Group (2012), *Ensuring Fair, Affordable and Safe Financial Products for Vulnerable Users*, Brussels: Financial Services User Group.
42 Ibid.

4
The Australian SACCs Appeal

Abstract: *The chapter on Australia looks at both the historical and more recent development of regulations, harmonizing the states and territories of the country. It details the specific issue of consumer credit and payday lending, in the context of a society that deregulated banks and also witnessed a growth in personal debt profile. It addresses the demand for high-cost credit, the extent to which other countries can learn from Australia, before looking at the development of ethical finance.*

Keywords: credit; debt; payday loans; regulation

Packman, Carl. *Payday Lending: Global Growth of the High-Cost Credit Market.* New York: Palgrave MacMillan, 2014. DOI: 10.1057/9781137361103.0007.

The regulation of the payday lending industry in Australia has long been of interest to those keen to advocate on behalf of strict interest rates and stringent governmental intervention. It has also increased its international interest after George Osborne, the chancellor of the exchequer of Great Britain, raised the country's regulatory regime as a good practice example at the time of his surprise move in support of a cap on the total cost of credit in 2013.

Of course naturally, there are similarities in Australia and Britain. It has been observed that owing to the follow-on effects of colonialism, the Australian legal system very closely aligns with the British system. In its more recent history Australian regulation over consumer credit was disjointed and in need of significant reform. In a short space of time the regime has gone from being fractured to something more uniform and some might argue the envy of other nations.

The development of uniform regulations over payday lending

From 2009 consumer credit was regulated under provisions in the National Consumer Credit Protection Act 2009 (NCCPA). Four years later saw the enactment of the Consumer Credit Legislation Amendment (Enhancements) Act 2012 (CCLAEA) which provided a national interest rate and further requirements for the advertising of consumer credit products. Prior to July 1, 2013 Australia had a state-by-state system with "patchwork" interest rate controls that differed by territories. New South Wales, the Australian Capital Territory, and Queensland had, for example, a rate cap of 48 percent, while Victoria had a 48 percent cap for unsecured loans and a 30 percent cap for secured loans, both excluding fees and charges. There were no limitations on interest rates in the Northern Territory, South Australia, Tasmania, and Western Australia.

The rise of the high-cost credit industry in Australia, and the careful attention politicians and consumer advocates in the country had been paying to the industry in the rest of the world, particularly the United States and the UK, highlighted the need for very targeted new rules and regulations. On September 21, 2011, the Federal Minister for Financial Services and Superannuation, the Hon Bill Shorten MP, introduced into Parliament the Consumer Credit and Corporations Amendment (Enhancements) Bill 2011 (Cth) which in turn proposed amendments to the National Consumer Credit Protection Act 2009 (Cth) ("NCCP Act") including reforms to lease lending, mortgage lending, and high-cost credit. The Enhancements Bill, importantly, addressed the growing desire to place caps on interest rates, fees, and charges, and prohibit the refinancing and rolling over of existing payday loans. It would be addressed in addition to an increase in the supply of affordable credit products such as microfinance and low and no interest community loan schemes.[1]

The Enhancements Bill was also the second phase of new consumer credit protection laws that attempted to harmonize existing state and territory laws. The Australian Securities and Investments Commission (ASIC) went on to provide greater oversight and appease a call for increased consumer advocacy at a regulatory level. The bill also provided active response to the view that existing responsible lending obligation, catered for under the NCCP Act, was now insufficient in addressing borrower harm in the case of credit arrangements such as with payday loans.

At the same time as the bill's passage, there were growing lobbying attempts by representatives of the payday lending industry itself. Subsequent amendments to the bill and the ultimate version, which eventually passed in 2012, carried what some have considered being reduced protections for payday loan borrowers, indicating eleventh hour success by the industry in shaping the outcome. All in all, however, lenders that sell small amount loans, or SACCs (small amount credit contracts, that is to say unsecured loans of AUD$2,000 or less with a length of 16 days to 1 year),[2] in the updated regime will be prohibited from setting up contracts with borrowers deemed unsuited to such a product. The definition for suitability, comparably strict measured against many other countries with similar consumer credit markets, is one of standout points of the new regulation regime. Additional requirements made from 1 March, 2013, will ensure SACC lenders inquire about whether the borrower is currently in default under an existing credit contract; or has been a debtor under two or more SACCs in the last 90 days. Further still, inquiries will need to determine whether a borrower derives 50 percent of their income from social security payments. In such a case that person will be prohibited from taking on a credit contract that requires fortnightly payments of more than 20 percent of their gross income. Like any affordability assessment this is to ensure a borrower is not taking on more than they are likely to chew. Any breach of a lender's credit obligation could lead to a civil penalty of up to $220,000 for an

DOI: 10.1057/9781137361103.0007

individual,[3] and a possible two years in prison, and for $1,100,000 for corporations, partnerships, or multiple trustees,[4] based on the amount of penalty units incurred (e.g., for an individual in breach would receive 2000 penalty units at $110 per unit).

What is clear is just how prescriptive these changes are. Elizabeth McNess, the principal adviser of financial services at Choice, a not-for-profit consumer organization, pointed out at the close of 2013 that there has been an adverse impact on consumers and a growth in credit denial.[5] However, this isn't necessarily to do with the strictness of the rules, rather, the complexity of them. As payday lenders in the country come to be brought under new rules, with firm penalties, it is likely there is going to be immediate risk avoidance. It might be suspected that with the constant fight between lobbyists and consumer advocates to get the system they see as desirable, lawmakers have been pushed to compromise with something that is overly complicated. Problems recorded elsewhere, such as the UK, are felt to be because of regulation that is too loose, not too prescriptive. As it became apparent in Chapter 3 the UK's responsible lending criteria was implemented, and went largely unchanged, at a time when the financial environment was far less damaged and the increasing problem of lender malpractice, particularly by payday lenders, was less known. Because Australia's new rules were written after all eyes were on the global financial crash, and the problem of payday lending was better understood, it has a far more solid focus.

What Australia's regulators now need to continue tightening is enforcement of existing laws. It is all well and good having a range of new regulations and expectations of an industry that is famed across the western world for its, to say the least, relaxed attitude to sticking with guidance, but this counts for nothing if enforcement of law shares this relaxed approach. It has been noted in the Regulation Impact Statement that before the changes, when only a few states and territories had interest caps of 48 percent, lenders in Queensland and New South Wales avoided the state regulation by including contractual terms to avoid the statutory definition of a credit contract and requiring borrowers to purchase additional goods as a precondition to obtaining a loan. A favorite of some lenders, which I was reminded of by Gerard Brody, the CEO of the Consumer Action Law Group, the foremost consumer advocacy group in Australia, was the obligation of borrowers to purchase financial literacy DVDs, clearly a means by which lenders were recouping lost revenue in a relatively tighten regulatory system.

The concern by groups such as Consumer Action is that now, with a more uniform approach to price capping, incidents of circumventing the regulations will increase, jeopardizing the efficiency of new rules. But their concerns don't stop here. As of July 1, 2013, fees charged on small amount loans less than $2,000 are capped and limited to a maximum amount. Lenders are obliged only to charge a one-off establishment fee of not more than 20 percent of the loan amount; a monthly account keeping fee of not more than 4 percent of the loan amount; a government fee or charge; and default fees or charges (the credit provider is lawfully unable to collect more than 200 percent of the amount loaned if you default). If the new rules on fees and charges still seem high that will be because they are. As Consumer Action pointed out in 2012, while pleased with the bill that eventually passed through the House of Representatives it was hoped that with the announcement of what they considered a weakened comprehensive cap on fees and interest, that's to say a cap set higher than they would have hoped for, they had hoped "this would be offset by 'complementary measures' which would effectively address the unsafe aspects of this type of lending." Instead, they go on to argue in a press statement, "we have a cost cap set at the level proposed by Australia's biggest payday lender—the cost of loans will come down, but short term loans will still have interest rates that most Australians would consider outrageous—up to 240 percent per annum."[6] Debt traps, they conclude will not be a thing of the past—far from it.

From February until March of 2014 the Australian government gave the opportunity to interested groups and bodies to consult on draft legislation and explanatory materials that will enhance consumer protection for those Australians who borrow payday loans. The Consumer Action Law Centre teamed up with the Consumer Credit Legal Centre to prepare a joint submission, in which they pledged support for a general antiavoidance provision in the national credit laws.[7] They also sought to find a way to simplify the existing law. It was suggested in the submission that the credit limit of $2,000 in the definition of SACCs means that the consumer receives no more than $2,000, not including fees and charges, as opposed to $2000 as a total cap. This, the submission continues, has the benefit of preventing small amount credit providers "from charging the maximum fee for such contracts where they are arranging for a consumer to enter into a new continuing credit contract each time the consumer requires a further advance." While of course this appears, at first glance, like a mere battle of words—a regular occurrence when contemplating regulatory change—it actually regards something rather serious that demonstrates a very mature discussion on the regulation of payday lending, which is absent in many other countries: what mechanism is in place to ensure a lender doesn't act upon the profit incentive to charge the most they can in fees once those fees are capped?

Detailed analysis of the new Australian pricing system for small amount loans shows that a potential loophole would be for a lender to, at the point of setting up a new advance to an existing customer, terminate (or indeed allow a borrower to terminate) a credit contract in order to immediately create a new one, thereby entitling that lender to charge the maximum rate for establishing a new credit contract. Even as regulation over this type of consumer credit evolves, more questions will be raised to tighten up the approach. To be sure, however, nobody could deny how far it has come.

The background of the Australian consumer credit regime

A 2012 Social Impact Report stated that having access to consumer credit is considered to be one of three key measures of financial inclusion in Australia, in addition to a basic banking product and basic insurance. Lack of access either to any of these three products indicates immediately that the individual is financially excluded. But the form in which that credit took has changed significantly over the years in the country.

Until the 1980s installment credit was dominant for consumers. Hire purchase could often be relied on by low and medium income households to finance goods, though the lender–borrower relationship was not without its tensions. One of the anomalies in hire purchase, back in the early twentieth century, was that regulation tended not to favor the consumer. Since the hirer, in a hire purchase agreement, was not a buyer so to speak, and no bill of sale was agreed, contracts could be terminated at any time, leaving the hirer in a quandary since the Bills of Sales Act and Sale of Goods Act did not apply. That was until the introduction of the Hire Purchase Acts in the 1930s, which addressed lack of regulation over this kind of credit.[8] Outstanding hire purchase balances in the late 1930s were the equivalent of 2.5 percent of total gross household income at that time, which works out at around the same as the UK. It was then in the 1960s that other more sophisticated credit products broke through the market. Outstanding consumer credit in total remained steadily at the equivalent of 15 percent of household income during the period of 1960 to 1995, rising only to 20 percent after 2005.[9] What was rather peculiar then was that all existing regulations providing oversight to consumer credit, as stated, were repealed to make way for the Credit Act 1984—which didn't actually include Credit Unions, Building Societies, or trading banks despite the fact that by 1986 they supplied between them around 80 percent of total credit. This important, if rather ironic, oversight was only rectified in 1996 by the introduction of the state-based Uniform Consumer Credit Code (UCCC) 1996.

A situation familiar to many other advanced countries at the time, inflation started to increase in the 1970s, which the Reserve Bank of Australia (RBA) had to address. Monetary controls were still imposed on banks but not on nonbank financial intermediaries such as hire purchase companies. Since such companies came to be known in the country as the second banking system the lack of proper control over them was regarded as both unfair and undermining monetary controls. Eventually the Financial Corporations Act 1974, which intended to bring nonbanks in within that framework, came into being. What occurred after then were efforts to do away with interest rate ceilings providing banks with the ability to compete on level playing field with other financial institutions.

By the early 1980s it was central bank policy to increase interest rates, which in turn reduced the take up of consumer credit. However, by 1934 deregulation, which was spurred on by a 1981 inquiry by the committee led by Sir James Keith Campbell, assisted the big four banks (the National Australia Bank, the Commonwealth Bank (CBA), Westpac, and Australia and New Zealand Banking Group, or ANZ) to consolidate their position in the consumer credit market. Many nonbanks, also, converted to become banks at this time.[10] After this time there was an incredible growth of consumer credit.[11] As academic Margaret Griffiths has suggested this was due to many factors: a change in social attitudes to debt and relative wealth growth which saw people borrowing against future earnings, but also a significant decline in growth rates of income resulting in credit use as a means of maintaining living standards.[12] Of course, as well Griffiths notes, there is nothing wrong with credit use per se, but this period gave rise to the issue of problem debt: the growth in use of debt consolidation and refinancing, evidence of debt arrears, bad debts, record number of bankruptcies, instability in employment market (identified as primary cause of consumer bankruptcies since 1992); altogether strongly suggests consumers not coping with debt servicing commitments.

Growth in outstanding debts, in the consumer credit market, has risen at an average rate of 12.6 percent every year. The total outstanding consumer credit debt rose some 560 percent between 1980 and 1996, from $33.3bn to $220.3bn.[13]

There would be no better prompt for regulatory attention to this fact. The UCCC came into legal effect in most Australian States and Territories on November 1, 1996. While many territories had moneylending acts in place since the forties, such as the one in Victoria adopted an interest rate cap of 48 percent in 1941, based on amendments in 1927 to the UK Moneylenders Act, the UCCC was at that point the most comprehensive set of regulations pertaining to consumer credit in Australia.

Two years later Australia's first payday lender was set up, which to begin with was not covered under UCCC regulations owing to short-term exemption.[14] In 2000 three firms, Cash Converters, Australian Money Exchange, and Cheque Exchange, were providing an estimated 100 credit transactions, per company, every month[15] and by 2001 around 82 payday lending businesses were offering approximately 12,800 loans a month[16]—some considerable growth of around 640 percent, particularly stunning for such a new industry. As the industry developed in Australia so, too, did the demand for greater amounts of high-cost credit. In 2002, only 6 percent of loans were in excess of $500. By 2008, this had grown to 39.9 percent.[17] According to research carried out by the Consumer Law Action Centre, in terms of the principal lent, the payday lending industry saw a growth of around 973 percent between 2002/3 and 2008/9. In that time the average loan size had increased by some 51 percent. Rather notably, the 2008–2009 principal loaned figure represented a small reduction from 2007/8 and was the first year since 2002/3 in which the business declined, which may have been the outcome of a comprehensive interest rate cap of 48 percent in Queensland on July 1, 2008.[18] Between 2005 and 2009 alone, Cash Converters reported a customer base of 92,927 rising to 231,262. In 2013 the company boasted a 12 percent increase in profit on the year previous of $32.9m. They had, however, reported a 46.4 percent slump in profit in the first half of 2013/14, to $9.9m, which it believes had to do with a tightened regulatory regime. Interestingly, revenue was up 15.5 percent to $155.8m in that same period. One representative told the press that: "improvement has been driven by our customers becoming more familiar with the documentation required to meet the new regulator requirements."[19]

A review of high-cost credit, like payday loans, carried out by Infosys Technologies Ltd in 2008 found that at that time the payday lending industry was worth a total of $800m in value.[20] On closer examination the figure derives from Business Review Weekly writer Jane Searle's 2007 article "Cash in Demand"[21] which, as has been previously pointed out,[22] provides no breakdown but is consistent with similar statistics and is likely to represent a rough estimate of the volume of loans lent. Clearly what can be suggested here, common to many other countries (such as the UK for instance), is that the recording of loan volume from the payday lending industry needs more regulatory attention.

In the years since 2009 when movements toward tighter regulation gained pace and bad practices, particularly in the payday lending industry, have been paid more attention, regulators have been attempting to crack down on rogue operators. Wasting no time after significant modifications to the law beyond 2013 ASIS had already banned 20 individuals for operating without a license or trying to engage in irresponsible lending. The regulator brought about court actions, the most notorious of which involved a company using a bogus diamond trading scheme to circumnavigate credit laws.[23]

In September 2013 a leading Australian payday lending firm, the appropriately named Cash Store, became tied up in a legal battle with ASIS for breaching credit standards. ASIC filed for civil penalties in the Federal Court on claims that the firm was involved in what they described as predatory lending, allowing and facilitating unaffordable loans to customers who had relatively low income levels, the maximum penalty of which, in this instance, would be $340,000.[24]

One of the major improvements to the consumer credit regime was made with regards to advertising. The Australian Government, since the National Consumer Credit Protection Regulation 2010,[25] requires all lenders selling standard home loans to give customers a Key Facts Sheet when going about the necessary credit checking arrangements. A warning about small amount credit contracts is to be made on premises, and information that is headed "Do you really need a loan today?," which is actually a requirement of the National Consumer Credit Protection Act 2009, is included on the sheet. The fact sheet also contains the following details:

— For information about other options for managing bills and debts, ring 1800 007 007 from anywhere in Australia to talk to a free and independent financial counselor;

— Talk to your electricity, gas, phone, or water provider to work out a payment plan;
— If you are on government benefits, ask for an advance payment from Centrelink;
— Go to www.moneysmart.gov.au—MoneySmart shows you how small amount loans work and suggests other options that may help you.

On the sheets there is also information on how a borrower can cancel deductions made on their account at any time during a live credit contract. The details, which pertain specifically to deductions made from a salary, are the following: "Important: You can cancel this deduction request directly with your employer at any time. If you cancel this deduction request you will be in default if you do not make alternative arrangements to make repayments." Warnings on websites are similar.

Additional guidance on advertising made in 2012 also covers the following areas:

(a) balanced messages about the returns, features, benefits, and risks of the product or service, including warnings, disclaimers, qualifications, and fine print;
(b) fees and costs;
(c) interest rates;
(d) comparison rates;
(e) product suitability claims in advertisements, including responsible lending;
(f) nature and scope of credit assistance; and
(g) restricted terminology ("independent," "impartial," and "unbiased"; "financial counselor"; and "reverse mortgage").

Adverts are also legally obligated to have a prominent comparison rate of interest. The Cash Converters comparison, for example, shows next to the site's sliders that the user directs to specify how much credit they want to borrow, a comparison with a 6 month loan of the same amount to show the interest rate.

Once again, wasting no time, ASIC raised concerns that the payday lender Nimble Australia Pty Ltd, previously known as Cash Doctors and one of Australia's largest online lenders, was displaying potentially misleading advertising. According to a press note by ASIC in both 2012 and early 2013 Nimble made statements on its website and in the press that its credit contracts were "short term," failing to clearly explain that their product was a continuing credit contract with an indefinite term.[26]

They were not alone. One study on several firms offering online payday loans including Nimble, Cash Store, and Cash Converters, found in August 2013 that their websites still had many areas of concern, particularly regarding the positioning of warnings on websites which were either not clear or that would not attract the attention of a browser, incomplete text, and in some instances did not have to be looked at by consumers before getting to the application stage.[27]

When speaking to Professor Paul Ali at the Melbourne Law School, himself an expert on the Australian payday lending industry, he told me that so far the payday loan "health warnings," as they are known, apply only to physical stores and websites of payday lenders. As yet none of the TV advertisements for payday loans carry equivalent health warnings, which is surprising given the sheer volume of payday loans adverts in Australia, particularly during sports coverage.

The demand for the payday loan product

What is absolutely clear, looking at the growth of the payday lending industry in Australia, is that there is a high demand for a short-term credit product in the country. One of the reasons reported by respondents of a 2012 survey for taking out loans was insufficient income to meet basic living expenses.[28] Indeed the historically high levels of Australian household debt over the past decade have culminated in very successful fringe finance sector.[29] While clearly this has not been a problem for higher income households, who in large part will be developing greater assets and in any case will be more financially resilient, low-income households taking on more debt to sustain an acceptable way of life is bound to be a significant problem. While it is very encouraging that household incomes have grown on average 63 percent more than the cost of living since 1988, according to one report,[30] what this doesn't tell us is the impact poverty has had. In 2010 the poverty line, based on 50 percent of the median income for a single adult, was $358 per week. For a couple with two children it was $752. Around 265,000 people (12.8 percent of all people) in 2012 were living below the poverty line; 62 percent of people below the poverty line had social security as their main income and 29 percent had wages as their main income. The environment for an industry that relies on the custom of low-income people underserved by mainstream banks is ripe for the picking.

However, the payday loan customer has not been described in these terms by everyone. A 2008 study by independent research body Policis[31] found, for example, that half of borrowers taking out payday loans have household incomes of more than $35,000 per annum and a quarter have incomes of more than $52,000. Furthermore, payday borrowers are more likely than other credit users to be in full-time work. While at face value these figures tell us something very interesting and frightening, namely that many people taking out loans are from working households, indicating that in-work borrowers are struggling with cash flow problems as well, the findings by Policis are rather widely contested.

Their research divides people up into four discrete segments: Payday Mainstream; Mainstream Excluded; Mainstream Strugglers; and High Income Convenience Users. They find that most of the loan users they deal with in their research data fall into the first category of payday mainstream, that is someone with modest level use of both nonstandard and mainstream credit and little problem debt; 45 percent of high-cost credit users fall into this camp. The next down the list, 25 percent of users, are those with relatively high incomes who use payday loans out of convenience. Only 19 percent of users fall into the mainstream excluded category, those with relative financial exclusion who try to avoid revolving credit, and at the bottom of the list is mainstream strugglers, making up 12 percent, who have seriously adverse credit histories.

The research also highlights another interesting aspect, that of the relative benefits of using a payday product rather than a credit advance on a credit card. As is pointed out the share of income represented by debt service for payday users is the same as that for low-income borrowers taking cash advances on credit cards: 20 percent. Immediately a question arises: it has long been suspected of the payday lending industry that it could not survive were it not for the high-risk borrowers who are more likely to be repeat customers. Not only are we told in this report that the most frequent user of payday loans is someone with modest use of mainstream credit and payday loans, but we are also told that there is no evidence suggesting that borrowers are trapped in cycles of debt. As it is put rather bluntly: "Few borrowers are ... exposed to additional costs other than that implied by the headline price of the loan."

This of course contradicts one of the most influential studies on payday lending in general, by Mark Flannery and Katherine Samolyk.[32]

They asked in 2005 whether an industry like this could survive if there were fewer high-frequency borrowers. Their answer is that it might, but its long-term scale would be substantially decreased. The incentive for this industry then is to keep high-frequency borrowers borrowing. Are we really to suppose that the growth of payday lending in Australia has occurred off the back of modest use and not repeat use? Additionally, are we really to suspect these findings are accurate when we know from Cash Converters' own data that 46 percent of borrowers were in receipt of government benefits and 75 percent of those customers had an income under $36,000?[33] This is not the only suspicion about the Policis report. In their 2010 examination of the payday lending sector the Consumer Action Law Centre pointed out that the Policis paper, as well as a number of others,[34] was commissioned by Cash Converters, even though the papers themselves do not report the commissioning party.[35] The main criticism about the research, however, is that the reports do not provide raw numbers for survey results or disclose survey questions. The suspicion being that there is little to prove one way or the other whether the questions were leading or whether the sample size the data assessment is made on is representative.

The influential 2012 report Caught Short,[36] which has as its focus a cohort of people that have taken out payday loans while in receipt of Centrelink payments, that is payments from the government's welfare agency that pays a range of services for retirees, the unemployed, families, carers, parents, people with disabilities, finds details that somewhat contradicts the Policis report. Over half the respondents reported taking out more than 10 loans in the last two years. Within this group three quarters had taken out more than 20 loans. As opposed to so-called "Payday Mainstream" borrowers less than 7 percent of respondents owned a credit card and over 60 percent had a poor credit rating. The question then becomes how are so many loans being taken out by those most financially excluded when Policis report so few borrowers struggle? Further still, 10 loans over two years is considered high enough, but the cohort of people taking on 20 loans over that time is demonstrably in a debt cycle. With around 20 percent of the Caught Short sample engaged in spiraling, or the refinancing of a partially paid-out loan to start a new loan and 25 percent simultaneously taking two or more loans from the same or different lenders, we can see clear differences in the findings of researchers from the University of Queensland and the Royal Melbourne Institute of Technology, and that of Cash Converters-backed reports from Policis.

One of the telling findings of the Caught Short report, as well as Zac Gilliam's report for the Consumer Action Law Centre, cited above, is the frequency of poverty and low incomes among participants and those surveyed. In one report it was observed that 85 percent of borrowers had an income less than two thirds of average weekly earnings. In Gillam's research this figure is at the much lower rate of 51 percent. It has been suggested by the authors of Caught Short that this is because of the profile sample of some of the participants. For example, nearly a third of participants in the Gillam study stated they had a university degree, which is proportionally higher than the 23 percent of working-age Australians that hold a university degree.[37]

The other main point from the Caught Short is the figure that less than two in five respondents had ever taken out a bank loan. The reasons, when asked, given by respondents were either that they would never expect to receive a bank loan upon request, or that their credit ratings were poor. As the report notes, again contrary to the claims of the Policis report, "[o]ver 60 per cent of borrowers talked of having a 'bad' credit rating or a 'black mark' recorded against their name by Veda—an Australian credit rating agency controlled by Macquarie Bank."[38]

Payday lenders and their industry bodies may look at this and suggest (very reasonably, on the face of it) that what speaks here is not the frequency of low income in receipt of their loans, but those who are good payers, those borrowers who are able to take out loans and pay them back on time or without eventually defaulting on a loan. Indeed back in 2011 this is just what Cash Converters' managing director, Peter Cummins, did. One counterargument, more convincing than Cummins', is that the true price of a payday loan is seldom shown in default rates alone. When taking out a loan with Cash Converters, for example, borrowers have to give access to what is called a direct debit where the lender is able to take out prearranged sums as repayment. In other instances, notably private renting for example, where payments are made out of someone's salary, at the point where they have to pay they realize they cannot afford the bill, or cannot afford to repay one bill without running the possibility of going without food or paying for other bills, then a repayment plan would be arranged. With the type of access to an account that is arranged when taking on a payday loan, a repayment plan is not required and indeed the risk is that a lender will drain a person's account without recourse to a payment plan that can allow the borrower to reprioritize their outgoings, meaning that they will not necessarily have to go without food or other household necessities such as heating. After all, the lender legally holds responsibility here when they arrange a loan based on an affordability assessment. And a responsible lender will set up a repayment plan on the realization that circumstances have changed to the detriment of the borrower. Some lenders will not happily reschedule a loan. Cash Converters have said that they would reschedule loans for struggling borrowers, however Matthew Drummond, an editor of the Australian Financial Review, inquired about taking out a loan from a store in Melbourne in 2011,[39] only to find that the store representative mentioned only the late payment fee while saying nothing about a free reschedule. It is for reasons like this, and many others, that now Australia has tightened its rules over payday lenders, it needs to ensure the enforcement of those laws are carried out rigorously.

The supply of payday loans

The Caught Short report has to date the best description of how payday lenders see themselves and the role they play in Australian finance. In the interviews with lenders, undertaken by the researchers, it was pointed out that in the main they emphasized due diligence in lending, claiming that they recognized the difficulties experienced by people in relatively tough economic times, and that payday lenders were advancing finance to borrowers who were otherwise unfulfilled by mainstream lenders. They also highlighted the need to match the risk of those lenders with a higher premium, given the propensity of default rates among this group.[40]

While the report points out that no evidence was provided to back up the claim, lenders maintained that if "genuine" reasons such as the loss of employment or some other major circumstance changed led to a nonpayment, then they would be prepared to renegotiate favorable conditions than for what they felt were nongenuine reasons such as money spent on gambling or tobacco—though quite why a lender would even be considering a loan to supplement these things rather than referring them to debt advice or financial counseling is beyond me. In fact, rather tellingly, on the topic of counselors, the report notes that lenders prefer to negotiate directly with clients rather than outside parties, counselors being one case in point, who lenders saw as "unhelpful."[41]

Lenders profess to provide a quick and easy service and in large part claim they offer everything a bank cannot. One lender from the Gold Coast in Queensland told researchers: "We endeavor to treat our customers very, very well. As a generalization we behave as unlike a bank as we possibly can." While lenders are likely to see what they provide as a good, rational choice made by people with open options with credit, counselors were less likely to agree with this, arguing instead that consumer advocates critical of payday lending, and critical of a business model based on trapping people in debt to ensure a pool of return custom, are closer to the mark. Indeed as the report goes on to say, when interviewed counselors mentioned "not financial choice, but pure economic necessity."[42]

Counselors were more likely to give examples of loans that facilitated borrowing cycles and a high proportion of loans being made to borrowers who are identified as low income and vulnerable, have ailments such as mental illness or a lack of education. Even if efforts by lenders are made to discourage their product, it gives an interesting insight into this type of credit. As the report's authors point out: "We know of no [other] business model that discourages customers from purchasing their product."[43]

Many consumer advocates would argue that tighter regulation and greater penalties in place has forced the hand of payday lenders to be more compliant with the law. When I spoke with Phil Johns, the chief executive of the National Financial Services Federation (NFSF), Australia's main payday lender trade body with members such as Cash Converters, he told me that the work of the regulator, ASIC, has resulted in improved moneylending businesses that are no longer financially incentivized to practice outside the rule book. "From 1 July 2010, for the first time ever," he said, "this regulatory compliance set up by the very active regulator ASIC came backed with criminal code penalties for providing credit to someone who cannot afford to repay it." While not taking a view necessarily about these changes, he did say the ball is now in the court of his industry's critics. "This [the changes to the regulation] addressed all issues anti-industry campaigners raise such as debt spirals. Simply, no-one who spends tens of thousands of dollars to set up a shop, then just as much to purchase a credit license, is going to give anyone a $500 loan they cannot afford to repay, only to then face criminal code penalties for a $500 loan to consumers."

Johns suggested to me that there is a rise in ALICE customers (or, asset limited, income constrained, employed) visiting his members for loans.

He pointed out that: "Three years ago these consumers would have been considered bank-only people, but due to the identical laws and licensing requirements in Australia and the banks continuing to raise the minimum value of a personal loan, which is now around $5000, it now makes no difference to a consumer if they walk through a bank or small amount credit provider in Australia—the process and the protections are the same."

Johns gave rather even-handed critique of the regulator when I spoke to him. He dislikes the rogue lenders as many of us do, in fact from his perspective they do little to help the representation of his industry in general. I assumed, on the face of it, that he would support the changes to the role and strength of the regulator. But it may be no surprise to find out that he has not always been so diplomatic. In spite of the criticism by consumer advocates that the new uniform pricing rules are not strict enough, particularly with regard to fees charged, Johns and the NFSF came out in the press saying: "While, on the face of it, the cap on fees and charges proposed by Minister Shorten (The Hon Bill Shorten MP, leader of the Labor party) may seem like a good thing, the cap is at a rate below the cost of providing a short-term loan. It will hurt hundreds of thousands of ordinary Australians already financially excluded from the banks and credit unions." Despite the fact that Cash Converters, a member organization of Johns and the NFSF, campaigned and lobbied for a relaxation on the fee cap, Johns opposed them on the grounds that lenders would not be able to operate with them in place.

The NFSF took to a campaigning effort. The "No cap" online campaign run by Australia's largest payday lender, Cash Converters, used the names, addresses, and images of thousands of customers.[44] Borrowers had their photographs taken and a dedicated website was created for advertising on the Cash Converters website. The campaign, by some, may be seen as an addition to the company's acknowledgement of the importance of loyal, repeat custom, while others are more suspect of what that loyalty means.[45] It is interesting to see that in 2011 Cash Converters went to press to say that a cap on interest rates is not an imminent threat to its business.[46] This was even after a drop of 12 percent in Cash Converters' share prices, from 78 to 68.5 percent. Only after a cap was decided did the company come out to say changes will impact, perhaps negatively, upon their business operations. An example costing of the cap on $100 over a month will include $24 in fees and interest, but given the monthly flat rate of 4 percent the loan will be $28 if the duration of the loan is one month and one day.[47] As previously mentioned, to break down a loan like this would include: a one-off establishment fee (of not more than 20 percent of the loan amount); a monthly account keeping fee (of not more than 4 percent of the loan amount); a government fee or charge; and default fees or charges (the credit provider cannot collect more than 200 percent of the amount loaned if you default—that is, fail to pay back the loan). Whether the claim that payday lenders are unable to operate with a cap like this is disingenuous is a subject returned to in detail in the discussion chapter, though it is worth considering the consequences of a loan at unlimited terms, or without a cap on fees associated with it, as Mike Symon, Federal member for Australian Labor in Deakin, did in a 2012 speech to parliament when speaking about a payday loan borrower who had taken out a loan of $170 from Cash Converters in 2011: "Three years later, and after 64 loans, the debt had ballooned out to a grand total of $15,450, including $5,407 in fees. Allowing for the fact that the money was always due in a month, the annualized interest rate on each loan was about 425 percent."[48] If this is how profit maximization is achieved then perhaps the wider societal and economic costs ought to be considered.

Building up alternative finance

When I spoke to CEO for Consumer Action Law Centre Gerard Brody in 2012 about payday lending he was quick to remind me about improving access to affordable credit and schemes that with Government investment have developed such as the No Interest Loans Scheme, which is a loan scheme of up to $1,200 with no interest or fees, and Step Up, a not-for-profit loan developed by the National Australia Bank and Good Shepherd Youth & Family Service, where loans for between $800 and $3,000 are available for low-income families and made at a basic interest rate of 3.99 percent, per annum. When I mentioned these loans to Phil Johns at the NFSF he made his opinions on the organizations known: "The Brotherhood St Laurence and Good Shepherd Youth and Family Service are not financial institutions, they are consumer advocate and support groups, *attempting* [my emphasis] to provide, in some cases, limited for specific use, low cost credit...these organizations for the last 10 years or so, have not been able to consistently run the provision of these alternative loans without issue—as the well-intended staff/

volunteer staff in these organizations simply don't know the first thing about running a lending business."

Johns also mentioned to me that there is a portion of the Australian population that these organizations, and large banks in the country, are unable to cater for. On this he has a point. But then this may historically have been to do with the regulation of credit unions. Howell and Wilson in their paper on the role of credit unions to address financial exclusion, for example, say that in the recent past a concerted effort to make credit unions run more like banks has sullied their ability to contribute meaningfully to addressing financial inclusion. Operationally this has been all the more difficult by the regulatory system treating credit unions as banks in regard to their capital adequacy ratios, or in other words the relatively high (and perhaps untenable amount, particularly for small, community-based credit unions) amount of capital required by the regulator. Howell and Wilson's criticism here is that this ignored the mutual structures of credit unions and prevents their operating without significant external support.[49]

Academic Race Mathews made the point that historically credit unions originated in postwar Australia because of a need for affordable personal loans for furniture and household appliances, away from predatory moneylenders.[50] In today's Australia, with the extraordinary rise of payday lenders, only relatively few credit unions are able to compete. One lender that Howell and Wilson talk about in their study is the Fitzroy and Carlton Community Credit Union, one of the few mainstream credit providers in Australia willing to provide small loans to people on low incomes, including those in receipt of Centrelink payments. The motivation by the credit union to provide a small loan, and benefit from the support of the credit union for budgeting, consumers "are able to achieve goals and improve their position."[51] Critics might point out that while this is well meaning it really doesn't answer the question of whether, in general, credit unions have the means to cater for a riskier customer who may not be able to save (it should be noted that primarily credit unions are savings institutions).

Certainly their part in bringing about greater financial inclusion is at best ambiguous. So much time has been spent both on tackling the predatory lending of payday lenders, and equally on bringing regulation up to speed insofar as it concerns credit unions, not enough time has been spent linking these two work streams together. From July 1992 the Australian Financial Institutions Commission launched the Financial

Institutions Scheme, under which Non-bank Financial Institutions, including credit unions, were required to comply with certain prudential standards including, as previously mentioned, capital adequacy. At this stage in the regulatory development, as Howell and Wilson make clear, credit unions were required to hold 15 percent of their assets in liquid form under this scheme, compared with the 6 percent that banks were required to hold, impacting significantly on their longevity and survival. The authors point out that small "grassroots" credit unions were driven out of business, while new ones were prevented from forming.[52] Regulation was supposedly improved by the uniformity of capital requirements for credit unions and banks alike, mentioned above, under the Wallis Inquiry Reforms and the establishment of the Australian Prudential Regulatory Authority (APRA) on July 1, 1998. This, along with the requirement for credit unions, under Uniform Consumer Credit Code and the Financial Services Reform legislation, to disclose material requiring a very large investment by industry in printing, freight, training, postage, and time, makes operating a credit union very labor intensive indeed.

To date, in the Australian Treasury's "Strategies for Reducing Reliance" there included some ideas for reducing reliance on payday loans including changes to emergency financial relief provided through Centrelink, improving access to hardship provisions for borrowers in financial difficulties, and strategies to expand and improving access to alternative credit schemes. However, no specific government policies have been announced to reduce the reliance of vulnerable borrowers on payday lending, or to build up the ability and resilience of the credit union sector to incorporate customers once seeking payday loans as their only option.

In Australia some 3,123,519 people are either severely financially excluded or fully financially excluded. This accounts for around 17.7 percent of the population. In 2011 the figure of combined severely and fully excluded was around 2.65m.[53] The number is increasing, and these are the people who are the most likely to have to visit a payday lender. These are also the same people the Good Money Hub, which opened to the financially excluded in April 2012, sought after.[54] Quite clearly what is needed is more thinking about what role no or low-interest credit providers, that are committed to providing access to those previously financially excluded or those working poor who are consigned to taking on high-cost, expensive credit, that at once jeopardizes their ability to save and, even with a cap, sees more money disappear in expensive interest payments. It is worrying that with all the good thinking about how the Australian regulatory architecture can crack down on predatory lending, there has been so little evidence of how the supply of credit, once from a booming payday lending sector, can be replaced with something much more ethical, cost-effective for the consumer, and committed to the financial health of low-income communities.

To be sure there are hurdles for credit unions, balancing on the one hand the ability to be more like banks, with the responsibility that follows, while staying local and community oriented. Equally challenging is being able to take on a riskier customer base. Low- and no-interest schemes also have their own challenges ahead. One lender, for example, Fair Loans Foundation, in July 2013, had to pay back 854 of their borrowers the sum of $157,000 in overcharged interest following an ASIC enforcement. Owing to an error the company were advertising interest rates lower than the actual rates charged, alleging that Fair Loans advertised rates of 15.95 or 19.95 percent when rates were actually 28.25 or 35 percent. Phil Johns at the NFSF, who delighted in recalling this story when I spoke to him, claimed to personally contact the company himself to inform them of their error. It is rather rich of Johns to criticize Fair Loans Foundation. In a simple test of the online application processes of Fair Loans and Cash Converters, it will be found that when one borrows $1000 over one year from Fair Loans the total repayable amount, including fees, is $1,199.50 which amounts to an annualized percentage rating of 35 percent. When borrowing the same amount, over one year, from Cash Converters the total repayable cost will be $1,680, an annualized percentage rating of 152 percent.

Nevertheless a considerable mission to find an alternative supply of credit for payday customers is needed. Additionally the ASIC must seriously consider introducing a real-time database of loans taken out from payday loans stores in order to make the enforcement of their new rules that much easier. With a model like that of Veritec, a US-based real-time regulatory solution for the payday lending industry, ASIC could identify situations in which loans were underwritten by lenders who already have two existing loans on their record in the previous 90 days, as is prohibited in Australian law, thereby offsetting further examination of the company and possible penalty proceedings.

As is the case with many other countries, the Australian payday lending industry has broken through on the back of an increasingly dangerous debt economy, particularly damaging for low-income households, and preys on custom that the mainstream banking sector has failed to accommodate for. But the solutions, while radical, and the envy of many other nations, are only half done since there is so much left to do building up an alternative, more ethical, and community-based, supply of responsible credit. Enforcement of the law and ensuring lenders aren't able to increase avoidance activity—as is supposed they already are[55]—are the next big steps for ASIC.

Notes

1 Ali, Paul, McRae, Cosima Hay, Ramsay, Ian and Saw, and Tiong Tjin (2013), The Politics of Payday Lending Regulation in Australia, *Monash University Law Review*, Vol. 39, No. 2, pp. 412–451.
2 The CCLAEA, on July 1, 2013, introduced three different consumer credit definitions—small amount credit contracts (SACCs), medium amount credit contracts (MACCs), and short-term credit contracts (STCCs). A STCC is a loan for under AUD$2,000 with a length of 15 days or fewer. Interest is not allowed on these loans and is effectively banned under new legislation. SACCs are unsecured loans of AUD$2,000 or less with a length of 16 days to 1 year. Lenders can only charge establishment fees of 20 percent the adjusted amount and interest of 4 percent per month (which is 48 per cent per annum). Other fees, charges, and interest payments are not permitted on the loan. MACCs are loans for AUD$2,001 to $5,000 for between 16 days and 2 years. Lenders are entitled to charge interest of 4 percent per month (48 per cent per annum) and establishment fees up to AUD$400.
3 Rodbard-Bean, Anthony (2012), *Unsuitable Lending Under the Consumer Credit Protection Act 2009 (Cth)*, Melbourne: Foley's List.
4 See the Consumer Credit Legislation Amendment (Enhancements) Bill 2012. Available at http://parlinfo.aph.gov.au/parlInfo/search/display/display.w3p;query=Id%3A%22legislation%2Fbillhome%2Fr4682%22.
5 McNess, Elizabeth (2013), *The Australian Responsible Lending Act: The Verdict is Cautiously Optimistic for the Consumer*, in Consumers International, "Responsible Lending: An International Landscape," London: Consumers International.
6 Media Release: Credit Enhancements Bill a 'Win' for Payday Lenders, Consumer Action, June 27, 2012, http://consumeraction.org.au/credit-enhancements-bill-a-win-for-payday-lenders/.
7 Joint CALC and CCLC submission: Payday Lending Regulation, 2014. Available at http://consumeraction.org.au/wp-content/uploads/2014/03/Joint-CALC-CCLC-submission-payday-lending-regulations-Mar-2014.pdf.

8   Pvan der Eng, Pierre (2008), *Consumer Credit in Australia During the 20th Century*, Canberra: Economics and Econometrics.
9   Ibid.
10 Ibid.
11 Griffiths, Margaret (2008), The Sustainability of Consumer Credit Growth in Late Twentieth Century Australia, *Journal of Consumer Studies & Home Economics*, Vol. 24, No. 1.
12 Ibid.
13 Ibid.
14 Duggan, Tony (2001), Access to Credit in the Alternative Credit Market: An Australian Comparison, *The Canadian Business Law Journal*, Vol. 35, No. 3.
15 Ibid.
16 Howell, Nicola and Wilson, Therese (2005), Access to Consumer Credit: The Problem of Financial Exclusion in Australia and the Current Regulatory Framework, *Macquarie Law Journal*, Vol. 5.
17 Gillam, Zac (2010), *Payday Loans: Helping Hand or Quicksand? Examining the Growth of High-Cost Short-Term Lending in Australia, 2002–2010*, Melbourne Consumer Action Law Centre.
18 Ibid.
19 The West Australian, Cashies profit slumps on new regulations, *The West Australian*, February 17, 2014. Available at http://au.news.yahoo.com/thewest/business/wa/a/21512585/cashies-profit-slumps-on-new-regulations/.
20 Infosys Technologies Ltd (2008), Fringe Lending in Australia—An Overview, *National Australia Bank*. Available at http://www.nab.com.au/vgnmedia/downld/Infosys_Fringe_Lending_Study_PDF.pdf.
21 Searle, Jane, Cash in Demand, *BRW*, August 23–29, 2007.
22 Ali, Paul, McRae, Cosima Hay, Ramsay, Ian and Saw, Tiong Tjin (2013), Consumer Leases and Consumer Protection: Regulatory Arbitrage and Consumer Harm (2013), *Australian Business Law Review*, Vol. 41, No. 5.
23 Green, Shane, Watchdog takes aim at rogue operators in payday loans sector, *The Age*, November 17, 2013. Available at http://www.theage.com.au/national/watchdog-takes-aim-at-rogue-operators-in-payday-loans-sector-20131116-2xnwo.html#ixzz2vBXRSOk1.
24 Chandrashekar, Aparna, Australian payday lending firm in row over unethical lending, Payday Loans Digest, September 11, 2013. Available at http://www.paydayloansdigest.com/2013/09/11/australian-payday-lending-firm-in-row-over-unethical-lending/.
25 National Consumer Credit Protection Regulation 2010. Available at http://www.comlaw.gov.au/Details/F2013C00707/Html/Text#_Toc365554626.
26 Media Centre, ASIC concerns sees payday lender change advertising, *ASIC*, May 23, 2013. Available at https://www.asic.gov.au/asic/asic.nsf/byHeadline/13-112MR%20ASIC%20concerns%20sees%20payday%20lender%20change%20advertising?opendocument.

27 Consumer Law Action Centre (2013), *What Warning? Observations about Mandated Warnings on Payday Lender Websites*, Melbourne: Consumer Law Action Centre.
28 Banks, Marcus et al. (2012), *Caught Short: Exploring the Role of Small, Short-Term Loans in the Lives of Australians*, The University of Queensland.
29 Details of which are discussed in La Cava and Simon (2003), *A Tale of Two Surveys: Household Debt and Financial Constraints in Australia*, Sydney: Reserve Bank of Australia.
30 Phillips, Ben (2013), *NATSEM Household Budget Report: Cost of Living and Standard of Living Indexes for Australia*, Canberra: University of Canberra.
31 Ellison, Anne and Foster, Robert (2008), *Payday in Australia: A Research Study of the Use and Impact of Payday Lending in the Domestic Australian Market*, London: Policis.
32 Flannery, Mark and Samolyk, Katherine (2005), Payday Lending: Do the Costs Justify the Price?, *FDIC Center for Financial Research*, Working Paper No. 2005/09.
33 Symon, Mike, Consumer Credit and Corporations Legislation Amendment (Enhancements) Bill 2011—Pay Day Lenders, *MikeSymon.com.au*, June 26, 2012. Available at http://www.mikesymon.com.au/2012/06/26/consumer-credit-and-corporations-legislation-amendment-enhancements-bill-2011-pay-day-lenders/.
34 The other reports by Policis, commissioned by Cash Converters, are called *The dynamics of low income credit use: A research study of low income households in Australia* and *The impact of interest rate ceilings—the evidence from international experience and the implications for regulation and consumer protection in the credit market in Australia*. Both reports had the same authors.
35 This accusation is made on p. 25 of Gillam, Zac (2010), *Payday Loans: Helping Hand or Quicksand? Examining the Growth of High-Cost Short-Term Lending in Australia, 2002–2010*, Melbourne: Consumer Action Law Centre.
36 Banks, Marcus et al. (2012), *Caught Short: Exploring the Role of Small, Short-Term Loans in the Lives of Australians*, Queensland: The University of Queensland.
37 Ibid.
38 Ibid.
39 Drummond, Matthew, Debt Traps in Payday Loans, *Australian Finance Review*, June 1, 2011. Available at http://www.afr.com/p/national/debt_traps_in_payday_loans_spudnLHN7ig9RJKUKa97sK.
40 Banks, Marcus et al. (2012), *Caught Short: Exploring the Role of Small, Short-Term Loans in the Lives of Australians*, Melbourne: The University of Queensland.
41 Ibid.
42 Ibid.

43 Ibid.
44 Ali, Paul, McRae, Cosima Hay, Ramsay, Ian, and Saw, Tiong Tjin (2013), The Politics of Payday Lending Regulation in Australia, *Monash University Law Review*, Vol. 39, No. 2.
45 Gillam, Zac (2010), *Payday Loans: Helping Hand or Quicksand? Examining the Growth of High-Cost Short-Term Lending in Australia, 2002–2010 (2010)*, Melbourne: Consumer Action Law Centre.
46 AAP, Cash Converters says reforms not a threat, *Sydney Morning Herald*, June 1, 2011. Available at http://news.smh.com.au/breaking-news-business/cash-converters-says-reforms-not-a-threat-20110601-1ffe9.html.
47 The estimation made by Tim Boreham, the business correspondent for The Australian. Boreham, Tim, Payday's heyday over as lenders consolidate, The Australian, June 24, 2013. Available at http://www.theaustralian.com.au/business/companies/paydays-heyday-over-as-lenders-consolidate/story-fn91v9q3-1226668458714#.
48 Symon, Mike, Consumer Credit and Corporations Legislation Amendment (Enhancements) Bill 2011—Pay Day Lenders, *MikeSymon.com.au*, June 26, 2012. Available at http://www.mikesymon.com.au/2012/06/26/consumer-credit-and-corporations-legislation-amendment-enhancements-bill-2011-pay-day-lenders/.
49 Wilson, Therese and Howell, Nicola (2007), Be Careful What You Ask For: What Role Now for Credit Unions in Addressing Financial Exclusion in Australia?, *Griffith Law Review*, Vol. 15.
50 Mathews, Race (1998), Credit Unions and the New Mutualism, *The Journal of Co-operative Studies*, Vol. 30, No. 3.
51 Wilson, Therese and Howell, Nicola (2007), Be Careful What You Ask For: What Role Now for Credit Unions in Addressing Financial Exclusion in Australia?, *Griffith Law Review*, Vol. 15.
52 Ibid.
53 Connolly, Chris (2013), *Measuring Financial Exclusion in Australia (2013)*, Swinburne: Centre for Social Impact.
54 The Premier of Victoria, Good Money hub to provide access to affordable financial services, Media Release, *The Premier of Victoria*, April 27, 2012. Available at http://www.premier.vic.gov.au/media-centre/media-releases/3825-good-money-hub-to-provide-access-to-affordable-financial-services.html.
55 Gardner, Jodi (2014), *The Challenges of Regulating High-Cost Short-Term Credit: A Comparison of UK and Australian Approaches*, UK: Centre on Household Assets and Savings Management.

5
Back in North America

Abstract: *This chapter looks at how the high-cost credit industry has grown in a contemporary context. It discusses the wider points of the US consumer revolution, the part played by that revolution in raising the amount of dangerous debt for a growing population, a close look at the academic studies that have dealt with the issue of high-cost credit and payday lending over the recent years with the suggestion that because the industry in the United States is far more bedded in the consumer credit environment it has provided a great source of information for academia. The chapter also compares the United States with Canada to see the extent to which the industry has taken hold there.*

Keywords: Canada; consumerism; credit; credit unions; debt; post office; United States

Packman, Carl. *Payday Lending: Global Growth of the High-Cost Credit Market*. New York: Palgrave MacMillan, 2014. DOI: 10.1057/9781137361103.0008.

Revolutions come and go, some succeed for a little, some fail, but there is one revolution that has truly stood the test of time: The American consumer revolution. Lendol Calder has said that "since the 1920s the most crucial element in the pursuit of the good life has been access to consumer credit."[1] As we have seen in previous chapters this is what marks the United States out from many other countries, including many in Europe after World War II. However, the desire to consume on borrowed income has risen substantially over the years, even before the war. Writing in 1955 Raymond Goldsmith found that in every year after 1896 personal debt increased at rates well ahead of the rate of population.[2] A year after in 1956 the urbanist and journalist William H. Whyte starkly pointed out that "Thrift now *is* un-American."

As Calder also noted, indebted Americans of the1990s, at the time of his writing, are different from American debtors of the 1790s and the 1890s, but, he added, not completely different. The same can be said of course for the indebted Americans of the 2010s. The difference is in the many different types of debt obtainable now as well as the normalization of individual overindebtedness. Access to a good life may once have been sought through access to consumer credit throughout the years, today passing through an America of the subprime mortgage crisis, which in turn spurred on the most severe of recessions, consumer credit might not get you the life you wanted but the opportunity to pay the bills. Calder's point is to show how credit and debt have always been there, it is nothing new, but more Americans today will feel powerless and trapped in debt, from an array of lenders, not just the lenders providing who previously oversold predatory subprime loans to struggling households.

We have previously seen the changing emphasis in Europe from pro-debtor bias to pro-creditor bias, a consequence of the deregulation of banking in the Second Banking Directive of 1989 that Robert Guttmann and Dominique Plihon have argued was coupled with the United States to change the power dynamics in the credit system in general. An upshot of this was record high interest rates in the 1980s reaching 20 percent, which in turn forced US businesses into a period of prudent investment decisions, high technology, and financial-asset accumulation. In fact it is a familiar story the world over. As with the United States, the very same national conversation by politicians and journalists is being had in the UK on how to rebalance the shift away from low-skilled, low-paid, under-represented jobs with few progression paths, back to a heyday of relatively better paid manufacturing jobs, and other highly skilled professions where progression was more likely. Instead in both the United Kingdom and the United States, the world of finance was given a boost over other sectors, the consequences of which will be felt for years to come.

Interest rates, in both those countries, fell and in 2008 it was a record low of 0.25. However, the outcome of their record high, the subsequent changes to business investment, the decreasing share of wages for the majority of people in the labor market, and the drop-off of trade union representation meant that for many normal Americans even in time of relative recovery, what that meant to them on a personal, day-to-day level, was very little. In her chapter on the part that neoliberalism has had in creating the subprime borrower in Martin Koning's The Great Credit Crash, Johnna Montgomerie notices a sudden but prolonged change in the levels of indebtedness for those who would be most affected by fluctuations of the nature just described, low-income households, young adults, and senior citizens. Using figures from the Federal Reserve Board-sponsored Survey of Consumer Finances it confirms the assumption that the toxic mix of financial deregulation, and the continued financialization of low-income households, expressed in a declining wage share but growing subprime debt profile, had a downward effect on households from which they have never fully recovered.

From consumer dream to debt spiral

A Census Bureau Report showing household debt figures from 2000 to 2011 found that in this period more broadly the share of Americans holding some form of debt dropped from 75 to 69 percent. From this we might deduce risk aversion by banks, particularly in those latter years. However, it was also found in the same report that unsecured debt including from credit cards and student loans had risen for all US households from $5,365 in 2000 to $7,000—a 30.5 percent increase.[3] Mirroring similar trends across the world the need for credit continued as recession hit. In 2011 checking accounts became annually overdrawn, with almost 8m holders having to pay at least six overdraft fees per year, 4m paying more than 12 per year, and 2m paying 20 or more, with a cost of over $700 in fees.[4] If any more proof were needed credit was taken out, but not to fund the good life, but to line the pockets of creditors.

In fact the more debt that was taken on the less was being put back into the economy—the cost of people not being able to get through to the end of the month on wages alone has an effect, not just on the individual for whom debt is a living reality, but to the rest of society, too. A study of homeowners from 2007 to 2009 found for example that despite growing incomes of those homeowners their spending patterns were smaller, suggesting that their leverage weighed on consumption above and beyond what would have been predicted by wealth effects alone.[5] It was soon realized that this very same thing, with debt overhang, was happening more generally to people as they got caught in debt. A Federal Reserve paper from 2007 found that households with the highest debt-burdens were more sensitive to changes in income.[6] Reflecting the time, as more Americans started to take on more debt the problems associated with money being sucked out of the economy was soon realized, particularly when more debts were with nontraditional lenders. A study for the Center for Responsible Lending in 2003, just 10 years after the first payday loans in the United States began their circulation, found that fees on payday loans were costing families a conservatively estimated $3.4bn annually.[7]

The problems associated with payday lending became far more pronounced. As well as the so-called "mom-and-pop" operators lenders of this type of credit flooded the market. Nine out of 10 according to the Center for Responsible Lending run almost 50 percent of stores, Cash America with 660 locations as well as the biggest online operations, DFC Global (Money Mart) with 300 storefronts and operations all over the world, EZCORP (EZ Money) with 450 stores, First Cash Financial Services (First Cash Advance and Cash and Go) that carries out payday loans and pawning, QC Holdings (Quik Cash) with 450 stores, as well as Advance America which partners with Cash America online, Ace Cash Express with 1,700 retail locations, Check Into Cash owned by W Allen Jones which recently bought the UK payday lender Cash and Cheque Express, and CNG Financial (Check 'n Go) which also deals now in car-title lending.

A total of 12m Americans use payday loans,[8] and it has been estimated that 5 percent of all US citizens have taken out at least one loan.[9] Lenders have over 20,000 stores nationwide,[10] and are selling loans that on average cost 35 times that charged on typical credit card loans and roughly 80 times the rates on home mortgages and auto loans.[11] The average loan across the United States where they are not prohibited is $375 and typically repaid in two weeks.[12] John Caskey has pointed that the average two-week $200 loan can cost around $30 which is 390 percent (15 percent for two weeks multiplied by 26).[13] Between 10 and 20 percent of those loans are calculated as losses by lenders, which though as he points out is lower than might expected, the true cost other than what is taken out of the economy in debt overhang and interest repayment is never seen; if that same individual were able to take on a loan of a more reasonable rate and repayment then how much in financial resilience would that give them?

Though ensuring borrowers stay on as good customers for the high-cost credit industry, and not through traditional lenders, is big business in itself. The market of borrowers termed the "underserved" in 2012 generated around $89bn in fee and interest revenue from a volume of approximately $792bn in the principal loaned and other services. This was up on the following year in 2011 by 8 percent.[14] In a survey by the Federal Deposit Insurance Corporation it was found that of those who populated the unbanked population in the United States, 21.4 percent were black, 20.1 percent Hispanic, and14.5 percent American Indian.[15] African Americans it has also been found are significantly more likely to have some type of debt (94 percent) compared with the general population (82 percent), and this group are also one of the five most likely to be payday loan borrowers (including those without a four-year college degree; home renters; those earning below $40,000 annually; and those who are separated or divorced).[16]

Studies on the payday lending industry

Given that the payday loan originated in the United States it is hardly surprising to find that the most work, particularly academic work, has been carried out there in order to understand it better. Some familiar themes, common to many territories with a growing payday lending presence, occur. For instance, in looking at who it is that makes up the borrower of a payday loan (or small dollar credit [SDC] as they refer to it) the Center for Financial Services Innovation (CFSI) found in their survey of 1,100 small-dollar credit (SDC) consumers, plus an additional 500 non-SDC consumers for comparison, that borrowers tend to be less educated and concentrated more in the South of America.[17] The Credit Research Center in 2001 found that of their sample half recorded household incomes of between $25,000 and $50,000, with the other half almost equally divided by incomes of under $25,000 and over $50,000.[18]

On the question of whether borrowers were entering contracts unfit for them without their knowing, Ronald Mann recorded in his survey of 1,374 payday loans borrowers (for which the response rate was 96.5 percent) that around 60 percent accurately predicted how long it would take for them to pay it back.[19] On the other hand, Pew in their research on payday loan borrowers found evidence to suggest that even when some borrowers fully comprehend the terms and conditions of payday loans and know they will be difficult to repay, they will still take them; 37 percent of borrowers responded in their survey saying they would have taken a payday loan on any terms offered.[20] Nathalie Martin in an empirical study of borrower conduct found by and large a deep misunderstanding of the true cost of the loans payday borrowers were taking out.[21] Broadly speaking, while there is conflict between whether borrowers are in full knowledge of the loan contract, what is perhaps most worrying is that loans would be taken out regardless of their terms, speaking to general desperation of some borrowers' circumstances.

Studies found the extent to which the loans borrowers were being sold were inappropriate for them, given their financial circumstances. In one of their first studies on the industry the Consumer Finance Protection Bureau found that rather than being a temporary solution the majority of payday loan borrowers remained in debt an average of 212 days of the year.[22] Even in an earlier survey from 2001 carried out by Ellihausen and Laurence it was reported that 40 percent of payday loan customers rolled over on more than five loans in the previous 12 months, while 10 percent of the borrowers rolled over on an existing loan more than 14 times.[23] In a further study by Brian Melzer he found that rather than smoothing over incomes for many borrowers the debt burden caused them to fall behind on other payments.[24]

Skiba and Tobacman focused their attention on 51,636 biweekly paid borrowers who among them collectively took out 335,376 loans over a four-year period from 2000 to 2004. They found that with the first three loans there is a very elevated probability of default at around the 12 percent level, with subsequent loans being less risky to the point where default probability levels even out at around 6 percent.[25] In another paper Agarwal, Skiba and Tobacman find similarly, this time using credit scoring data from FICO and Teletrack, that taking out a payday loan predicts nearly a doubling in the probability of serious credit card delinquency over the next year.[26]

Not exclusively, but many of the studies that emerged after the initial heightened consciousness around high-cost credit and payday lending found that for a particular type of customer a payday loan can do real financial damage. The same customer who also brings in the most revenue given the increased risk of rolling over. In light of this, US policymakers and state legislators reacted in a number of different, but interesting ways.

Federal policy

Payday lending is regulated at the state level with varying policy responses for the existence of short-term loans, which will be discussed further on. For example, on a federal level the Truth in Lending Act (TILA) requires various disclosures, including all fees and payment terms, under the jurisdiction of the Federal Trade Commission. The Dodd–Frank Wall Street Reform and Consumer Protection Act gave the Consumer Financial Protection Bureau specific authority to regulate all payday lenders, though it does not have authority over interest rates at a state level. Furthermore, the Military Lending Act of 2007 imposes a 36 percent rate cap on payday and other loans such as tax refund loans (where a loan is made on the anticipation of a tax refund) or auto-title loan made to active duty armed forces members and their spouses or partners.

Payday loans according to FDIC, which can also be referred to in the United States as deferred deposit advances or small-dollar loans, are unsecured loans that borrowers promise to repay out of their next paycheck or regular income payment (such as a social security check). Because they are considered by FDIC as extensions of credit in their 2003 Guidelines for Payday Lending,[27] they are monitored by federal consumer protection law. At a federal level high-cost credit outlets selling payday loans have to accept review and comply with acts written into federal law such as the Community Reinvestment Act, on matters related to antidiscrimination, and TILA, of which Regulation Z requires lenders to disclose accurately all relevant information such as APR that will be considered by a consumer when weighing up the merits of a loan.

When the Consumer Finance Protection Bureau (CFPB) was first authorized after the passage of Dodd-Frank its director Richard Cordray pointed out that the most pressing matters for him and the bureau were mortgages, credit cards, and student loans. Shortly after payday loans were added to the list. Anecdotally it is known that supporters of the CFPB would like there to be more uniformity among states on what issues can be focused on regarding payday loans. Pew Research, a think tank that has concentrated a lot of resources in understanding what payday lending can mean for US households, points out that there is a "growing recognition of the need to shift back to affordable lending policies for all small-dollar loans." The Uniform Small Loan Law, after being adopted by a vast majority of states in the early twentieth century, was mostly phased out in the middle of the 1990s in order to accommodate for the single payment small-dollar loan. However, Cordray having noted that the regulation of interest rates was out of his hands, one of the first pushes made by the CFPB was on rollover loans. Further after the bureau was set up and the positioning of the CFPB becomes more concrete[28] there was a wider interest in online lending.

According to figures by Stephens Inc., the financial services company, it was estimated that online lending had grown rapidly from less than $2bn in revenue in 2006 to $4.3bn in 2012.[29] Contemporary disagreements have arisen around Internet lenders over whether they have to abide by laws of the state they lend in. As Gary Rivlin described it, "the internet, with its crannies and shadowy alleyways, provides another place where payday lenders can hide from the law."[30] In 2011 the SAFE Lending Act was passed in the 112th Congress requiring online lenders to abide by the regulations of the state in which the borrower resides. But the argument that had not yet been settled played on a far more emotive topic.

It has been argued that because of the geographical location of many tribes in the United States, which can be a barrier to economic growth, Internet-based companies are a positive boon. Taking into context the matter of Tribal Sovereignty, many online lenders are associated with tribes. It has been suggested that since tribal lending relies on "Congressional tolerance," that a future Congress could be more favorable to the CFPB pursuing online lenders with the support of businesses and consumer groups for a limited tribal immunity. Having said this in a private conversation one economist at the CFPB denied that they would raise this particular issue any time soon. Though, perhaps they will not have to: In March 2014, a US District Court brought a victory for the Federal Trade Commission after saying that predatory payday lenders will no longer escape federal regulators by claiming tribal affiliation. A 2013 ruling that the FTC can regulate certain companies associated with tribes may be the "fork in the road" moment.

State regulation

A total of 14 US states and the District of Columbia prohibit payday loan shops altogether, either directly or indirectly by making the type of short-term lending associated with payday lending technically unviable; 35 states, however, have introduced legislation that sought to overcome the Uniform Small Loan Law of 1916. In those states where it is not prohibited there are an array of different laws that regulate it. For example, in Virginia there is a capped number of times that a payday loan can be taken out and a cooling off period to allow time for personal financial organization of one day after pay, 45 days after a fifth loan is taken out, and 90 days if a pay plan is set up with a lender. In Washington, where there is also a cap of five times a loan can be taken out, there is a maximum loan amount set at $700 with a loan term of 45 days. In Illinois there can be granted a week's cooling period after being in debt for 45 days.

Some states have ways in which to record how many times a person is taking out a loan through a real-time database including Michigan, Illinois, Indiana, North Dakota, New Mexico, Oklahoma, South Carolina, and Virginia. Florida has the Veritec system, previously mentioned in Chapter 3. In 2002, the year Florida employed the Veritec system, it had around 940 stores that made 3m loans. To counter the idea that using the model has made payday lending any more a presence in Florida in 2011 it had over 1,500 stores that made nearly 8m loans. According to Nathan Groff, the Chief Government Relations Officer for Veritec Solutions, the number of lenders offering credit in Florida ever year has increased.[31]

The Milken Institute, looking at California, points out that it first authorized payday lending in 1996 to allow small loans of up to $300 for a maximum of 31 days with a restricted fee charge at 15 percent of the check amount. While lenders are barred from lending to customers who have loans outstanding with them there is no limit on the amount of times a customer can rollover on a loan. While the volume of storefronts went down from 2,445 in 2005 to 2,119 in 2011 the loan volume that those stores lent rose between $2.6bn and $3.3bn.[32] Florida has demonstrated that though there is a regulated measure of how many people are taking out loans at any given time, with a traffic light system that tells lenders and the regulator when they've got to a high number, the number of shops does not mean the state has rolled back its governance; equally California has shown that even if the number of shops decreases this is not a sign of loan volume going down, the reverse is true.

There is a similar point to be made about length and type of loans on offer. In their research Pew have suggested that the lifting of laws in 35 states to allow lump-sum repayment loans has meant more people survive on a knife-edge, often paying back in one go up to a third of their monthly income.[33] The Center for Responsible Lending has shown that installment lending is not always the best alternative: in some states where the installment loan is more frequently seen in payday loan storefronts the cost to take them out can be as much as a loan with multiple renewals anyway.[34] There is a middle point, though, that can be implemented more widely around the states that allow for payday lending. In Colorado lump-sum loans were reintroduced and back in use by 1992, on the cusp of the formalized payday loans industry coming into being. There was a $500 maximum loan amount, maximum number of outstanding loans of one, maximum rollover number of one, and finance fees of 20 percent for amounts up to $300. However, in 2010 a compromise was made with the lenders in the state that they could sell credit to borrowers in installments, not lump-sum, with terms of up to six months. As a result loans are borrowed for an average of 4 percent as opposed to the more typical 36 percent. They remain relatively expensive, but not quite as expensive as they once were.[35]

The Canadian payday loan outlook

Until 2006 payday loans in Canada were limited by usury laws of 60 percent per annum and were considered a criminal act under section 347.1 of the Criminal Code of Canada. After 2006 the code was amended to allow all nine provinces regulate the industry as they saw fit. Since then only Quebec and Newfoundland left it as it was, while New Brunswick specified a legal framework for payday lenders but have not as yet enacted it. The seven additional provinces all have rate caps at between 21 and 23 percent. In an early study Professor Iain Ramsay found that payday loans were particularly popular in Canada. Loans were generally made for around 14 days and cost around $15–25 per $100, or between 390 and 650 percent. The average loan provided to borrowers was $250. In a survey conducted by Money Mart it was found that 58 percent of payday loan customers were male with a median age of 32. Some 82 percent of borrowers earned $40,000 or less, 20 percent were classified professional, 18 percent skilled trades, and then between 12 and 4 percent for laborer, retail clerk, and restaurant/hotel worker. A similar outlook as many US states.[36]

In 2004 it was estimated that around one in every thirty-two people have used a payday loan at least once and that the industry was worth more than a billion dollars per year.[37] US companies quickly took advantage of the take-up of payday loans. Pennsylvania-based DFC Global (Money Mart) expanded its storefronts and online operations across Canada as did Texas-based Ace Cash Express who lend to Canadians online through Zippy Cash.[38] In a relatively rare signal that there was direct competition between banks and high-cost credit sellers, research carried out by the Bank of Canada found that communities with more bank branches and payday lenders per capita had a far more relaxed attitude to lending, including to already highly indebted households, which in turn brought about a greater amount of bankruptcies.[39]

The Criminal Code Act limits the size of payday loans to $1,500 and requires the loan period to be fewer than 62 days.[40] Additionally, the Canadian Payday Loan Association, which represents over 40 companies in the country, has signed up to stopping rollovers altogether. Stan Keyes, a former Liberal Party politician and as of 2006 the President of the Canadian Payday Loan Association, has said that "it was a very big decision, a very expensive decision, but there's a right way of doing things and a wrong way,"

Similar to the United States, Canada historically restricted products like payday lending until the demand grew so much that changes were made to the law to allow provinces to make of the industry as they saw fit. All but one has made it possible for the industry to grow in the country. In a departure from similarity to its US neighbors, it took for the payday lending association itself to put an end to rollover loans.

Alternatives

It is fair to say that the evidence of the alternative finance supply, from credit unions and other community banks, the verdict on their ability to meet the needs of the financially vulnerable is mixed. It is also fair to say that alternative finance is lacking in the United States. Alternative financiers themselves would agree. When banks aren't assisting payday lenders, as has been the remit of Operation Chokepoint, then they are selling payday loans. The CRL report on banks that had sold deposit advances found loan sales extended to individuals for a total APR of 225 percent. At this stage it would be incumbent to point out that another type of finance is required, but there are some home truths to be told about the activities of credit unions, that is a common theme across the world. As Victor Stango, the associate professor at the University of California, writing for the libertarian think tank Cato Institute found in 2012: "Credit unions have locations and business hours that consumers find less convenient than those of commercial payday lenders... At lower fees credit unions are either deterred outright from offering payday loans or are only willing to offer a type of loan that potential borrowers find unappealing."

The first credit union in the United States was founded in 1909 by Alphonse Desjardins, the cofounder of the Caisses Populaires Desjardins (now the Desjardins Group). Because of him a vast number of credit unions emerged during the depression. In 2003 credit unions that were covered by community reinvestment policy outperformed federal-chartered counterparts 69 percent of the time. They were subject to a rapid rise from 1990, when they numbered 244, to 2004 totalling 1,023. They were well known for lending to people on low incomes and had borrowers on their books that had incomes of 80 percent below the median. Community Development Credit Unions (CDCUs) have also been around since 1930.[41]

More so than in other parts of the world credit unions are well known for being business-oriented, as well as community focused in spirit. However, that conflict has resulted in many criticisms of the way in which it operates. For a period in 2009 the National Credit Union Administration (NCUA) required credit unions to report whether they offered payday loans. It caught the attention of the Center for Responsible Lending which promptly addressed the chairman of the NCUA, Debbie Matz, in an open letter requesting that she stop federally insured credit unions from making triple-digit payday loans, "by manipulating the APR, using third parties, or flying under the radar of enforcement."[42] It was found that some 58 credit unions were offering the loans, but stopped doing so after the publication of a National Consumer Law Center report highlighting the practice.

There has over the years been some concern that credit union, if there were to take on more customers who would otherwise be erroneously served by the payday lending industry, then prices will have to start reflecting theirs. Does this make the practice predatory? Many would argue that it wouldn't, since credit unions would also at the same time be offering services that payday lenders naturally wouldn't, such as debt advice and savings plans. Whereas payday lenders are far more profit-motivated, credit unions are focused on the community and so even if their pricing structure it wouldn't necessarily be from the same point of motivation. That, however, hasn't stopped researchers, agencies, and credit union staff from trying to design a credit product that could compete for the same custom base as payday lenders without having to charge what is not unreasonably seen as eye-watering rates of interest.

The Federal Deposit Insurance Corporation's Small-Dollar Loan Pilot Programme showed, albeit in a relatively small way, that payday-type credit products could be designed and sold without banks losing money in the process. LendUp, an online lender who still offer loans only at high rates of interest, does so with the term length being six months. Similarly Progreso made small loans to underserved Hispanics at more affordable rates. As it is there is still room for research on how small loans can be made without overwhelming low-income consumers with the sorts of prices payday lenders charges; however, some developments have been made with research carried out by the US Postal Service Inspector General into how the post office network could be utilized to the benefit of low-income borrowers is very promising but still in its infancy.[43]

Furthermore, a rapid development in 2013 of so-called "payroll loans" began to appear in Mexico, described as "small and relatively low-risk loans [that] help banks decide whether they want to deepen their relationship with a borrower in the credit equivalent of a coffee date."[44] These are similar to payroll deduction schemes found in many credit unions (including the UK National Health Service—the fifth largest employer in the world) where a loan is taken out by an individual and the principal and interest is paid for out of their wages. This in turn gives the creditor more security over the loan and dramatically decreases the risk of default. If a borrower should become in financial difficulty and seeks to prioritize payments then the same rules apply about staggering payments provided notice is given to the credit union. Despite the fact that there are small salary lenders in South America, for example the presence of

Dollar Finance in Mexico, the payroll loan seems the most sensible route to take. Wider uptake in all of North America would begin to take the toxic risk out of payday loan debts.

Notes

1. Calder, Lendol (2001), *Financing the American Dream: A Cultural History of Consumer Credit*, New Jersey: Princeton University Press.
2. Goldsmith, Raymond (1955), *A Study of Saving in the United States*, Vols. I and II, New Jersey: Princeton University Press.
3. United States Census Bureau (2013), *Household Debt in the U.S.: 2000 to 2011*, US: United States Census Bureau.
4. Borné, Rebecca and Smith, Peter (2013), *High-Cost Overdraft Practices*, in Center for Responsible Lending, "The State of Lending in America & Its Impact on U.S. Households", Durham: Center for Responsible Lending.
5. Dynan, Karen (2012), *Is a Household Debt Overhang Holding Back Consumption?*, Massachusetts: Brookings.
6. Johnson, Kathleen W. and Geng Li. (2007), *Do High Debt Payments Hinder Household Consumption Smoothing?*, Washington: Finance and Economics Discussion Series no. 2007-52.
7. Ernst, Keith, Farris, John, King, Uriah (2004), *Quantifying the Economic Cost of Predatory Payday Lending*, US: The Center for Responsible Lending.
8. The Pew Charitable Trusts (2012), *Who Borrows, Where They Borrow, and Why*, Washington: The Pew Charitable Trusts.
9. Ibid.
10. Ibid.
11. Barth, James R., Hamilton, Priscilla, and Markwardt, Donald (2013), *Where Banks Are Few, Payday Lenders Thrive*, California: The Milken Institute.
12. The Pew Charitable Trusts (2012), *Who Borrows, Where They Borrow, and Why*, Washington: The Pew Charitable Trusts.
13. Caskey, John (2005). Fringe Banking and the Rise of Payday Lending, In P. Bolton and H. Rosenthal (eds), *Credit Markets for the Poor*, New York: Russell Sage Foundation.
14. Center for Financial Services Innovation (2013), *2012 Financially Underserved Market Size Study*, Chicago: Center for Financial Services Innovation.
15. Federal Deposit Insurance Corporation (2012), *2011 FDIC National Survey of Unbanked and Underbanked Households*, Washington: FDIC.
16. The Pew Charitable Trusts (2012), *Who Borrows, Where They Borrow, and Why*, Washington: The Pew Charitable Trusts.
17. The Center for Financial Services Innovation (2012), *The Compass Guide to Small-Dollar Credit*, Chicago: The Center for Financial Services Innovation.

18 Elliehausen, Gregory and Lawrence, Edward C. (2001), *Payday Advance Credit in America: An Analysis of Customer Demand*, Washington: Credit Research Center.

19 Mann, Robert (2013), *Assessing the Optimism of Payday Loan Borrowers*, Columbia: Columbia Law and Economics Working Paper No. 443.

20 The Pew Charitable Trusts (2012), *Who Borrows, Where They Borrow, and Why*, Washington: The Pew Charitable Trusts.

21 Martin, Nathalie (2010), 1,000% Interest—Good While Supplies Last: A Study of Payday Loan Practices and Solutions, *Arizona Law Review*, Vol. 52.

22 CFPB Field Hearing on Payday Nashville, TN Tuesday, March 25, 2014. Available at http://www.responsiblelending.org/payday-lending/policy-legislation/regulators/OH-Remarks-CFPB-Field-Hearing-Payday-FINAL.pdf.

23 Elliehausen, Gregory and Lawrence, Edward C. (2001), *Payday Advance Credit in America: An Analysis of Customer Demand*, Washington: Credit Research Center.

24 Melzer, Brian T. (2011), The Real Costs of Credit Access: Evidence from the Payday Lending Market, *The Quarterly Journal of Economics*, Vol. 126, No. 1.

25 Skiba and Tobacman (2008), Payday Loans, Uncertainty, and Discounting: Explaining Patterns of Borrowing Repayment and Default, *Vanderbilt Law and Economics*, Research Paper No. 08-33.

26 Agarwal, Sumit, Skiba, Paige M., Tobacman, Jeremy (2009), Payday Loans and Credit Cards: New Liquidity and Credit Scoring Puzzles?, *American Economic Review*, No. 99.

27 FDIC Guidelines for Payday Lending. Available at http://www.fdic.gov/news/news/financial/2005/fil1405a.html.

28 It is anticipated that the CFPB will spell out in detail how they will regulate the payday lending industry in late 2014.

29 Online lending has grown rapidly in recent years—from less than $2bn in revenue in 2006 to $4.3bn in 2012, according to an estimate from the investment services firm Stephens Inc.

30 Rivlin, Gary, (2011), *Broke*, US: HarperBusiness.

31 Private conversation.

32 Barth, James R., Hamilton, Priscilla, and Markwardt, Donald (2013), *Where Banks Are Few, Payday Lenders Thrive*, California: The Milken Institute.

33 The Pew Charitable Trusts (2013), *Payday Lending in America: Policy Solutions*, US: The Pew Charitable Trusts.

34 Bocian, Davis, Garrison, and Sermons (2012), *The State of Lending in America & Its Impact on U.S. Households*, US: Center for Responsible Lending.

35 The Pew Charitable Trusts (2013), *Payday Lending in America: Policy Solutions*, US: The Pew Charitable Trusts.

36 Iain Ramsay (2000), Access to Credit in the Alternative Consumer Credit Market, paper prepared for the Office of Consumer Affairs, Industry Canada and the Ministry of the Attorney General, British Columbia, February 2000.

37 Mann, Ronald J. and Hawkins, Jim (2007), Just until Payday, *UCLA Law Review*, Vol. 54.
38 Bocian, Davis, Garrison, and Sermons (2012), *The State of Lending in America & Its Impact on U.S. Households*, US: Center for Responsible Lending.
39 Perkins, Tara, Bank of Canada Flags Lenders' Role in Consumer Debt, *The Globe and Mail*, January 4, 2013. Available at http://www.theglobeandmail.com/report-on-business/economy/bank-of-canada-flags-lenders-role-in-consumer-debt/article6930721/?service=mobile.
40 Kitching, A. and Starky, S. (2006). Payday loan companies in Canada: determining the public interest. Retrieved May 15, 2010, from http://epe.lac-bac.gc.ca/100/200/301/library_parliament/payday_loan-e/PRB0581-e.pdf.
41 Stegman, Michael (2007), Payday Lending, *Journal of Economic Perspectives*, Vol. 21, No. 1.
42 CRL Letter to Debbie Matz. Available at http://www.nclc.org/images/pdf/high_cost_small_loans/payday_loans/letter-ncua-cu-payday-may2013.pdf.
43 Office of Inspector General United States Postal Service (2014) Providing Non-Bank Financial Services for the Underserved: White Paper, US: Office of Inspector General United States Postal Service.
44 Guthrie, Amy, "Latin America's New Credit Frontier," Wall Street Journal, January 6, 2013. Available at http://online.wsj.com/news/articles/SB10001424127887323689604578222130866020660.

6
Discussion Points

Abstract: *This chapter attempts to bring about a discussion of the points raised in the previous chapters, on why the countries written about are uniquely placed to develop such a formalized high-cost credit industry, what kind of arguments have been developed in recent times about payday lending, as well as a detailed look into what has happened when the supply of high-cost credit has been reduced. It then goes over the common themes of the industry, its controversy, and how borrowers have interacted with it.*

Keywords: credit; credit unions; debt; loan sharks

Packman, Carl. *Payday Lending: Global Growth of the High-Cost Credit Market*. New York: Palgrave MacMillan, 2014. DOI: 10.1057/9781137361103.0009.

It has been necessary to limit the scope of this research to countries with a generally known formalized high-cost credit industry, for two important reasons: firstly it makes the research base more consistent than if it had included less formal instances of high-cost credit selling such as the Filipino "Bombay Five-Sixers," the micro-financiers in India who have turned to predatory lending, or the loan sharks of China.[1] While the study of these elements would be very worthwhile, my focus has been on the institutions that have grown specifically out of US salary lending and check cashing in to highly profitable businesses internationally. Providing boundaries to the research has allowed for a better comparison model from which to make general assertions about high-cost credit globally. The second reason is that what this study has looked at quite specifically is the political and economic grounds on which an industry can develop that targets working poor and credit-constrained individuals (though not exclusively), distinct from other forms of lending (or indeed other forms of consumer credit) where this might be expected more broadly from mainstream financial institutions.

Having demonstrated the research, policy, and evidence base, in the discussion that follows I put forward arguments and counterarguments around the question of high-cost credit, raise some key themes on the consequences of reducing the supply of high-cost credit, provide details of the commonalities that have occurred when looking at the global existence of a formalized high-cost credit industry, then discuss what the future of it may look like.

Arguments and their counterarguments for high-cost credit

APR argument: A very straightforward argument, where there is some agreement by consumer advocates and industry representatives. The Truth in Lending Act, as well as the Consumer Credit Act 1974 in the UK, stresses the need for the annualized percentage rate to be stated on any advertising or credit agreement to make sure that the borrower knows what they are signing up to. However, one point that would be made is that APR gives you an annualized rate for a loan contract that is typically going to be around two weeks. What consumer advocates and industry representatives in the UK both call for is an average price comparison to be stated when a loan is taken out. In Australia rules regarding payday loan adverts online, regulated by the Australian Securities and Investments Commission, a price comparison for six months and a more representative price is shown.

It is a competitive product, the market has spoken, there is demand: In her paper Payday Loans: The Case for Federal Legislation,[2] Pearl Chin points out that: "Empirical evidence...shows that competition among payday loans stores has not given any bargaining leverage to consumers." Why would this be? In a UK context Mary Portas, a high streets expert who carried out the Portas Review[3] for the Department for Business Industry and Skills found that while many retail shops were shutting down and high streets were looking progressively bare, some stores that were growing in number such as gambling shops and payday lenders were in a use class (which is the class order for town and country planning) that meant locally elected representatives could not oppose their setting up if it was perceived that there were too many in one place. More generally the professional services firm Deloitte found in 2012 that over the next five years four in 10 high street shops in the UK would close down.[4]

This is all the more worrying in the context of more research, this time by the Bureau of Investigative Journalism, which found that there was one short-term lender for every seven banks on the high street.[5] This in turn should be looked at in view of the 7,500 bank branches and building societies that have closed down from 1989 to 2012,[6] over which time payday lenders have grown from 0 to 1,427 shops in England, Scotland, and Wales. Is this good for competition? When competition has typically been raised in previous research it has been carried out in the context of what impact the appearance of payday lending has on perceptibly comparable credit products such as overdrafts, but the impact it will presumably have on the competition between payday lenders themselves will mean, not that prices will stagger downwards on the contrary, prices stay the same but the desire by the lender to get loans *out of the door*, quicker, so to speak, increases.

Something like this, for research purposes, may be rather difficult to quantify in an industry such as payday lending since it is apparent that toward profit maximization it has historically carried out minimal credit checking and affordability assessments in the underwriting process.[7] But it is not beyond the imagination to assume that if a payday lender wanted to appeal to consumers on the high street without changing its price structure, in a locality where payday lenders are more frequently seen, then promoting the speed at which they can underwrite a loan may be the best way for them, indeed that is why so many payday lenders advertise the speed of getting money into bank accounts, that's one of the few ways which payday lenders can actually compete with each other.

It is high cost to lend to the riskier customer: Ernst & Young were commissioned in 2004 to conduct a survey on the costs to a payday lending firm where they found that: "The operating costs of servicing new customers [on their first loan] represent over 85% of the total costs across the industry."[8] On looking at this survey it was suggested by McAteer and Beddows[9] that the high cost of a loan is carried by borrowers, not in fact by lenders who otherwise operate perfectly profitably. The argument then remains: if lenders were to lend in a way that reduced the risk of loan default (which isn't very much, a lot less than one might imagine. The Office of Fair Trading in the UK have said it is 14 percent[10] while one study from the US said it was between 10 and 20 percent[11]), which is the justification for the high pricing in the first instance, then the result would be a cheaper product for the consumer. Similarly as Skiba and Tobacman found in their four-year study with the first three loans there is a very elevated probability of default at around 12 percent with subsequent loans being less risky to the point where default probability levels even out at around 6 percent.[12] If pricing was based on this model then the payday lending industry would be very different.

The case for and against: Clarence Wassam, in his 1908 study on salary lending, pointed out that the "very fact that it is necessary for an individual to borrow to meet living expenses is evidence that it will be difficult for him to meet his obligations." As time progressed that view became lose. Consumer credit, as it has already been mentioned, can be worthwhile agreement to take when borrowed on the anticipation and deliverance of future prosperity. But this prosperity cannot be guaranteed now. Advocates of the payday lending industry will always say that they serve a need, and given the extent to which mainstream finance has pulled away from low-income consumers or those whom they feel too risky or damaging to their brand image, there is truth to this. But not all credit is equal; indeed not all credit is productive. Credit that is extended with the primary purpose of accumulating more money can be damaging if it is done without concern for those who are borrowing. But ought this type of loan be banned? Few people I suspect would answer yes to this. Short-term lending, with its associated costs, if it is the choice of the borrower is up to them. This type of credit, after all, would be filling the gap in the market that would be opened if it were banned. The problem we have, however, is that this product is seldom seen as the result of a free choice. Not necessarily that someone has been coerced into it, but rather that it was the last and final option an individual had.

What inevitably results from this thought experiment is we find that though something like payday lending perhaps oughtn't just be banned outright, it should be properly regulated. And it should be regulated in a way that stops lenders from running a business that has the primary aim of financially exploiting borrowers, who in turn require a cost from the rest of society (whether directly, that is to say in general taxation for health services because that person's debt anxieties have culminated in the need for media attention, in countries where that is applicable, or indirectly if that person now has less money to spend in the productive economy where jobs result). What results from proper regulation, however, is that a lender risks losing a key revenue stream. In operating *to the book* that lender is no longer able to extend credit to his target audience. What is the answer to this dilemma?

The argument concerning the reduction in supply: One very familiar argument by the industry is to say that if a government attempts to limit or cut off the supply, the result will be that credit access is far more difficult to access. In itself this is true. To take the statement *limit the supply* literally, this would mean access be harder. Furthermore, a frequent argument that an industry advocate may make is that this will push more low-income people into the arms of illegal loan sharks. However, as I will address, consumer advocates and critics of high-cost credit and the payday lending industry should not be overly perturbed by this line.

Illegal lending? Of all the industry's arguments, this one is the most frequently laid out. The Consumer Finance Association, a national body of payday lenders who oversee around 70 percent of the UK market, claim to have "exploded" a "payday myth" in saying that rather than caps being good for consumers, "caps create a market for illegal lenders." But a good deal of evidence suggests to the contrary.

If caps on credit have shown anything to be the case time and again it is that if a policy is issued placing a price ceiling on the amount that a high-cost credit lender lends, the price will gravitate up to that ceiling. When the state of Colorado legislature imposed a loan price ceiling in 2000 it was found that with the passage of time the average finance charge on payday loans edged toward the limit, and the variation in finance charges across payday loans has diminished.[13] This wouldn't indicate an industry governed by market rules that sees prices lowered by a greater volume of entrants. Before changes to the law in Colorado a $75 charge for a loan of $500 would be typical, and 96 percent of loans were made for the maximum fee permitted.[14]

But what is the evidence for illegal loans? The Consumer Finance Association goes on to say that "compared to the UK in France and Germany three times more low income households turn to illegal lenders."[15] This is from the same report by independent think tank Policis[16] that supposed price caps where they have used in other countries limits the access to credit in a way that leaves the door open for the black market. Professor Udo Reifner[17] responding to the statement not only goes on to say the difference is in fact greater than supposed (in 2004 use of illegal lending in the UK was recorded at 4 percent, France 12 percent, and Germany 10 percent), but what the report neglects to mention is the monopoly of credit that banks have in those other countries. In other words it is not the caps but the supply.

What I suppose we take from this is that since there is no evidence strong enough to suggest placing a cap on the total cost of credit that a lender can charge (to ensure against the raising of commission prices or fees), it has a direct knock-on effect for the business of illegal loan sharks, and caps are the only known intervention for bringing down the prices of payday loans, then as far as a responsible lending regime that is governed by sensible regulations go this is it. Taking stock of Professor Reifner's reply to Policis, however, there now needs to be some thinking around what an alternative supply of finance might look like in order to avoid a bank monopoly on credit.

The alternative supply and the meaning of community finance: Finance can and ought to serve as a corrective to the excesses of the capitalist world in which we live. If this seems slightly counterintuitive then it might be worth remembering that the word credit is rooted in the Latin for trust, indeed when we talk of community finance what do we evoke? In contrast to laissez-faire capitalism we might assume community finance can offer all that is good in society: relationships, cohesion, common bond, etc. Such a critique of the modern power dynamics within capitalism was very wisely first picked up by G.W.F. Hegel, and despite the Marxist reinvention in later years Hegel's point about capitalism was very different to the Left critique, namely in his acknowledgment that private organizations have emerged in the modern world with functions that could not be performed by the family or the state. Hegel also did not believe that capitalism would be overthrown by revolution, but where there are similarities between his argument and the classic Left critique is that capitalism, left to its own devices, would tear a person out of their local community and the family, and possess and consume them for its own purposes.[18]

For Hegel, when this happened intermediaries work to keep any semblance of order afloat and those intermediaries are represented by voluntary organizations and/or communities that have a vested interest in restoring and maintaining harmony and order. But what is significant about these intermediaries is that they exist alongside capitalism while acknowledging that in its purest sense it works against them; it is a corrective to capitalism rather than following its logic. In trying to understand what this might mean for social empowerment, at a time not only when the Berlin Wall has fallen and all that this means for the interplay of political and economic systems, but when most would accept that globalized capitalism is here to stay, we may wish to look toward the interstitial model for society.[19]

In accepting the above definition that the primary aim of capitalism pulls communities in an opposing direction of its need (pursuit of profit versus local cohesion and harmony) then the need for institutions built within the interstitial model, which build up a resistance to the forces and underlying motives of capitalism and acts as a harness for social empowerment in the niches and margins of capitalist society, becomes more apparent. Finance should reflect this interstitial model as closely as possible, and here is where the concept of usury becomes most useful: if the early (religious) critics of usury were motivated by the extent to which it tore apart communities, which in turn are key to building resilience of external factors (related to capitalism: poverty, boom, and bust), then for there to be a community finance it needs to serve as an alternative to the logic of capitalism as Hegel described it. If it fails to do this it takes on the logic of capitalism and ceases to be community-led, and for this reason it was right that the Center for Responsible Lending took aim at US credit unions selling payday loans; because payday loans, as they currently operate in so far as their business model has been described in previous research, work contrary to the logic of communities.

Reducing the need, indebtedness as standard, financialization, and neoliberalism: One of the main successes of the Occupy Strike Debt group, part of Occupy Wall Street and Occupy movements around the world, during its peak time around the financial crisis years was to expose the extent to which the buying and selling of debt is a dirty world indeed. In some circumstances loans are subject to debt sale in which the buyer has the right to collect the full amount. It has been found in a UK context that third-party debt collectors who pay around 10p for every £1 of debt expect to claim back around 20 percent of the owed money, but on that they will still have made a profit, this money being made on those who are struggling the most.[20] While legitimate, it is a perverse industry. Occupy in 2013 bought $14,734,569.87 in personal debt for just $400,000, then wrote it off.[21] The question is then the following: why can't this happen all the time? If the case has been made that growing overindebtedness is drawing money away from the economy, which then incurs a cost to the rest of society, then is this not a practice the government should be doing more often, rather than just groups like Occupy?

The answer is of course that the banks aren't always selling on their debts. In any case the debt for sale is only that of debtors who the banks have given up on. Default is a frequent issue of concern within payday lending as well so one option is to give individuals cheaper and more widely available options to declare as bankrupt.[22] Doing so can be very expensive, which is something for policymakers of countries that in recent times have seen an explosion of overindebtedness to look into—because to be sure allowing people to be in debt who really can no longer afford to be is not cheap either. Bankruptcy is never going to be an easy ride, and the costs and possible impact it can have on a person's credit record stop it from being a perverse incentive,[23] but the advantages are that when a bankruptcy order is made in most countries pressure is taken off the individual to deal with creditors, distress is reduced, a reasonable standard of living is allowed, and it gives a person a fresh start. These cannot be said for the person who is in debt-distress. It is important in this process to account for other forms of debt such as rental arrears.

When discussing emotive subjects as debt one response is not to find alternative means to sell that person credit, but the fight must be concerned primarily with wages and welfare. Others would suggest that the issue of tackling the root causes of debt, and an industry that only seeks to aggressively increase that debt for profit, go very much hand-in-hand. To that end, in this next part I identify and summarize those common themes that are associated with the high-cost credit industry, in order to better understand the motivation and values of it worldwide.

International commonalities

Debt and overindebtedness from which there was no return

- As Margaret Griffiths suggested a period in the early nineties in Australia gave rise to the issue of problem debt: the growth in use of debt consolidation and refinancing, evidence of debt arrears, bad debts, record number of bankruptcies, instability in employment market (identified as primary cause of consumer bankruptcies since 1992); altogether strongly suggests consumers not coping with debt servicing commitments.[24]
- From 1986 until 1990 unsecured lending rose in the UK from £24.2bn to £67bn. In the following 20 years it rose to £158bn making the UK one of the most indebted countries in the EU. Indebted households in the poorest households recorded debts of more than four times their incomes.[25]
- In the EU citizens were struggling to service their mortgages or consumer credit, and to pay their rent and utility bills. In 2010, more than one in four individuals reported that they felt at risk of becoming overindebted, while 11.6 percent were in arrears with payments related to such debts or bills (up from 9.9 percent in 2007).[26]
- Unsecured debt including from credit cards and student loans had risen for all US households from $5,365 in 2000 to $7,000—a 30.5 percent increase. In 2011 checking accounts became annually overdrawn, with almost 8m holders having to pay at least six overdraft fees per year, 4m paying more than 12 per year, and 2m paying 20 or more, with a cost of over $700 in fees.[27]

Deregulation with differing degrees of means to mitigate against it

- Deregulation in the 1980s in Australia which was deemed to be the cause of mainstream banks seeking to concentrate focus on more "profitable customers," the removal of interest rates, restrictions on lending and borrowing, and moves toward prudential guidelines and monitoring rather than direct control.[28]
- In the 1980s set about a radical economic policy marked out by 1986 for its so-called "Big Bang," the pursuit of deregulation in the financial markets that arguably resulted in the spurring on some of the effects of the global financial crisis of 2007–2012.

▸ In the United States the Depository Institutions Deregulation and Monetary Control Act in 1980, a reaction by the federal government to the rise in inflation, effectively overrode all existing state and local usury laws, giving way to the elimination of interest rate limits. This created the conditions whereby payday lenders could eventually partner with banks to sell high-cost loans to borrowers in states where such loans were otherwise prohibited.[29]

Neoliberal attitudes to welfare (private debt, especially consumer credit, not universal welfare, bringing prosperity)

▸ In Australia during the 1980s there was an incredible growth in consumer credit use. Many factors are deemed to be the cause: change in social attitudes to debt and relative wealth growth which saw people borrowing against future earnings. But also a significant decline in growth rates of income resulting in credit use as a means of maintaining living standards.[30]

▸ Critics have pointed various instances of welfare reversal in the UK. As the government made substantial budget cuts to local welfare assistance after the recession it was found that in many local authorities schemes designed to help those in the most need and/or on low incomes would have restricted access if they were deemed to be applicable for a consumer credit loan or able to borrow from friends or family.[31]

▸ In comparing the perception of consumer credit as an extension of welfare in France and the United States, it was found that in 1955, nonmortgage consumer debt averaged 15 percent of household disposable income in the United States, compared to 0.3 percent in France. In 2005 US nonmortgage household debt had risen to 23 percent of disposable income while French household debt was still below 15 percent of disposable income.[32]

Periods of ignoring the small gains made by high-cost creditors (growing in a quick amount of time unregulated)

▸ In Australia while key consumer credit legislation didn't cover short-term lending three firms, Cash Converters, Australian Money Exchange, and Cheque Exchange, were providing an estimated 100 credit transactions, per company, every month in 2000 and by

124 Payday Lending

2001 around eighty-two payday lending businesses were offering approximately 12,800 loans a month.³³
▸ From 2004 when the Department for Trade and Industry refused to accept there was a problem with the high-cost credit industry to the extent where they wouldn't look at changing laws on interest rate caps because it might build up illegal lending. Even in 2010 the government didn't want to break the "one-in-one-out" rule on regulations it had agreed to. In this time the payday lending sector grew exponentially.
▸ As Gary Rivlin points out, the Internet "with its crannies and shadowy alleyways, provides another place where payday lenders can hide from the law."³⁴ In this time online lending by payday lenders has grown to $2 billion in revenue in 2006 to $4.3 billion in 2012. US regulators demonstrably did not anticipate the gains that would be made in this area, though this has been hinted at as strong future consideration for the Consumer Finance Protection Bureau.
▸ As discussed in the chapter on Europe features of historical usury laws and interest rate restrictions may have impacted upon the ability of the high-cost credit industry making deeper gains in Europe, but one noticeable trend that has emerged is the opportunity for lenders, often offshore, to lend online or by SMS in countries with strict rate caps. They are able to do this by loading the costs otherwise derived from interest on to other charges such as commission. Holland was a case in point, though policy development that took place in 2012, blending some of the existing rules from the Consumer Credit Directive of 2008, has undercut industry gains.

Strategic interaction with national policy

▸ Throughout the 2000s, when only a few states and territories had interest caps in Australia of 48 percent, lenders in Queensland and New South Wales avoided the state regulation by including contractual terms to avoid the statutory definition of a credit contract and requiring borrowers to purchase additional goods as a precondition to obtaining a loan. These included the obligation to purchase "financial literacy" DVDs.³⁵
▸ The payday lending industry in the UK, in not interacting with the rules and regulations set out by the Office of Fair Trading,

culminated in the entire payday lending industry being investigated by the regulator. It was subsequently then referred to the Competition Commission. It was pointed out by the latter that "there are deep-rooted problems with the way competition works and that lenders are too focused on offering quick loans."[36]
▸ Brian Melzer in his study of credit access found using geographic data on payday lending locations compiled from state regulators that the number of store locations is almost 20 percent higher in zip codes close to payday- prohibiting states. This provided suggestive evidence that lenders were opening stores on borders to serve borrowers in states where payday lending is prohibited.
▸ Where it was possible to find information in an EU context it was clear that lenders had managed to circumvent existing usury laws and interest rate restrictions in some countries.

Commonalities of borrower interaction with the high-cost credit industry

Reasons for requiring high-cost credit

▸ In 2010 the poverty line, based on 50 percent of the median income for a single adult, was $358 per week. For a couple with two children it was $752. Around 265,000 people (12.8 percent of all people) in 2012 were living below the poverty line; 62 percent of people below the poverty line had social security as their main income and 29 percent had wages as their main income.[37]
▸ Polling by the think tank ippr showed that more than two out of five borrowers (41 percent) are using payday loans to pay for everyday expenses such as groceries. Almost a third of borrowers (32 percent) are using payday loans to pay utility bills, like gas and electricity, while one in five borrowers (22 percent) have funded Christmas presents and food. The polling also shows that more than a third of borrowers (35 percent) use payday loans in an emergency.[38]
▸ When the Center for Financial Services Innovation looked at the top three uses for a small-dollar loan product, among 1,100 surveyed borrowers, it included utility bills (36 percent of loans), general living expenses (34 percent), and rent (18 percent).[39]

Egregious collections practices

▶ It was found by Citizens Advice in the UK that one in three complaints to them in the first half of 2013 was about Continuous Payment Authorities (CPAs), where a lender is able to take money from a bank account as payment. While the lender is obliged to give the borrower notice of three days it has been found on numerous occasions that they hadn't, meaning that some people were left with no money in their accounts. A 2013 Office of Fair Trading compliance review found that across the sector firms were lending irresponsibly and engaged in business practices that harm consumers. It was deemed necessary by the OFT to refer the whole industry to the Competition Commission. CPA has been a consistently problematic issue (Office of Fair Trading, Payday Lending Compliance Review Final Report, 2013).

▶ In the United States Richard Corbray of the Consumer Finance Protection Bureau pointed to the ways in which payday loans companies engage in unfair collection activities, including: "using false threats, disclosing debts to third parties, making repeated phone calls, and continuing to call borrowers after being requested to stop." He also found that the same is true for debt collectors that work for payday lenders who "fail to honor the protections that are afforded to consumers through the Fair Debt Collection Practices Act."[40]

Rollover (loan sequencing)

▶ It was found by the OFT in their review of the payday lending sector that 28 percent of loans were rolled over which raised around 50 percent of the entire industry's profit. This is contrary to the claim by some elements of the payday sector that their business is for occasional use or one-off means to smooth over incomes. In response to this the Financial Conduct Authority has said they will limit the amount of rollover loans to two.[41]

▶ Gary Rivlin has described how this practice takes place in a US context, where "When [a] borrower renews [a] loan, the fees come out automatically... by the time borrowers get off this debt treadmill, they'll have paid much more in fees than their initial loan balance."[42]

Poor affordability assessments

▸ Verifying whether lenders are doing this is notoriously difficult without obligatory credit checking codes of conduct. The incentive certainly isn't there. While looking at the UK research group Europe Economics found that it may not be in a lender's best interests to conduct proper affordability checks which are time-consuming and expensive;[43] it has also been raised previously that lenders make their profit from repeat custom and rollover loans so there is a double incentive not to carry them out. Citizens Advice surveyed 4,140 consumers who had visited payday lenders, at the time under investigation from the regulator, and measured the results against the codes of conduct of the industry. While the codes said lenders should carry out an affordability assessment before the loan is extended, their survey found that over 65 percent of customers who were currently rolling over on a loan, a peak time to check affordability, said that the lender did not appear to check finances or general situation to see if they could afford the said rollover.[44]

▸ In Australia, a major report by the Consumer Action Law Centre described the payday lending industry as "providing a quick and easy loans service with limited administration and no credit checks." Looking more specifically at the online lending model, the report finds that "Online loan providers generally emphasize the speed, ease and convenience of obtaining a loan. The lack of a credit check is often used as a major selling point."[45] Policis interviewed payday loans users for a 2008 report looking at Australia, commissioned by Cash Converters. In a section aiming to show how taking on a payday loan does not compromise ability to afford essentials, they in fact unwittingly show poor affordability assessment practices: "Sometimes I had, you know, it's like, my gas is due at the same fortnight, at the same time that the Cash Converters is due. The gas and power, I've got to pay that. So sometimes I've rang up Cash Converters and said 'Look, can you make it next fortnight', and usually they go 'Yes.'"[46]

▸ In the United States the Center for Responsible Lending pointed out the practices that contributed to what they call the creation of the debt treadmill, one of which was the lack of underwriting for affordability, because the "payday lending business model depends on borrowers' inability to afford their loan and their subsequent need to borrow—paying more fees—multiple times."[47]

What is the future of high cost credit?

Return to installment loans?: The likely move more generally by the high-cost credit industry, if it hasn't done so already, is to move into longer term installment loans. There is evidence of this taking place in a very open way in some states of the United States. As an open letter addressed to Richard Corday of the Consumer Finance Protection Bureau by consumer advocates has pointed out the "payday loan industry is already in the process of changing the structure of its products in an effort to evade coming rules, without altering the fundamental problems of a dangerous product made without regard to borrower s' ability to pay."[48] The question is whether this is so bad? Longer term loans are frequently cited as preferable to many consumers and single payment loans have historically been cited as a problem for many borrowers to afford. As researchers at Pew have pointed out "Ensuring that borrowers can repay loans in installments over time will help alleviate the harms of payday lending. But," they continue, "unless policymakers also ensure that loans are structured according to the borrower's ability to repay…consumers will remain at risk."[49]

Car-title loans?: Already the risky loan practices of car-title lenders has been raised. In the State of Lending report by the Center for Responsible Lending[50] it was found that the way in which some of the loans are structured means that they can more or less guarantee that they will eventually repossess or eventually sell the car they've received as security. This is because the repayments are as a proportion of the average customer's pay, default is almost inevitable. Regulators in states such as Illinois and New Mexico report that car-title loan borrowers earn under $25,000 per year. Furthermore, it has been found that about half of all borrowers are unbanked.[51]

The Citizens Advice Bureau of the United Kingdom uncovered that logbook loans, which are loans secured on a vehicle, rose 33 percent between 2011 and 2014, with a 61 percent rise predicted to 59,286 overall.[52]

Notes

1. See Dunford, Chris, Are Moneylenders a Boon or a Scourge Upon the Land?, *Microfinance and World Hunger*, April 17, 2012. Available at http://microfinanceandworldhunger.org/2012/04/are-moneylenders-a-boon-or-a-scourge-upon-the-land/; Thirani, Neha, "Yunus Was Right," SKS Microfinance Founder Says, *New York Times*, February 27, 2012. Available at http://india.blogs.nytimes.com/2012/02/27/yunus-was-right-sks-microfinance-founder-says/; Barboza, David, In Cooling China, Loan Sharks Come Knocking, *New York Times*, October 13, 2011. Available at http://www.nytimes.com/2011/10/14/business/global/as-chinas-economy-cools-loan-sharks-come-knocking.html?pagewanted=all&_r=0.
2. Chin, Pearl (2004), *Payday Loans: The Case for Federal Legislation*, Illinois: University of Illinois Law Review.
3. Portas, Mary (2011), *The Portas Review: an Independent Review into the Future of Our High Streets*, UK: BIS.
4. Kollewe, Julia, Up to 40% of High Street Shops "Could Close Over Next Five Years," *Guardian*, March 20, 2012. Available at http://www.theguardian.com/business/2012/mar/20/high-street-shops-close-deloitte.
5. Warren, Tom, UK: One short-term lender for every seven banks on the high street, *TBIJ*, March 12, 2014. Available at http://www.thebureauinvestigates.com/2014/03/12/uk-one-short-term-lender-for-every-seven-banks-on-the-high-street/.
6. French, Leyshon and Meek (2013), *The Changing Geography of British Bank and Building Society Branch Networks, 2003–2012*, UK: The University of Nottingham.
7. A Citizens Advice survey from the UK where it was found 65 percent of borrowers were not asked about affordability. See: Citizens Advice, Payday lenders need to deliver on promise to check loans are affordable, May 15, 2013. Available here: http://www.citizensadvice.org.uk/_/press_office20130515.
8. Ernst & Young (2004), *The Cost of Providing Payday Loans in Canada: A Report Prepared for the Canadian Association of Community Financial Service Providers*, Canada: Ernst & Young.
9. Beddows, Sarah and McAteer, Mick (2014), *Payday Lending: Fixing a Broken Market*, UK: ACCA.
10. Straus, Rachel Rickard, Almost half of payday lenders quit the market rather than face OFT probe, This is Money, August 15, 2013. Available at http://www.thisismoney.co.uk/money/cardsloans/article-2393291/19-payday-lenders-quit-market-face-OFT-probe.html.
11. Caskey, John (2005), Fringe Banking and the Rise of Payday Lending, In Bolton, P. and Rosenthal, H. (eds), *Credit Markets for the Poor*, New York: Russell Sage Foundation.

12 Skiba, Paige Marta and Tobacman, Jeremy (2008), Payday Loans, Uncertainty, and Discounting: Explaining Patterns of Borrowing Repayment and Default, *Vanderbilt Law and Economics*, Research Paper No. 08-33.
13 DeYoung, Robert and Phillips, Ronnie J. (2009), *Payday Loan Pricing*, Kansas City: The Federal Reserve Bank of Kansas City.
14 Pew Charitable Trusts (2013), *Payday Lending in America: Policy Solutions*, US: The Pew Charitable Trusts.
15 Consumer Finance Association, Payday Myths Exploded. Available at http://www.cfa-uk.co.uk/payday-explained/payday-myths-exploded.html.
16 Policis (2004), *The Effect of Interest Rate Controls in Other Countries*, UK: Department for Trade and Industry, Hamburg: Institut Für Finanzdienstleistungen.
17 Reifner, Professor Udo (2004), *Comments on the DTI Study: "The Effect of Interest Rate Controls in Other Countries" (Germany, France and US): Preliminary Remarks from a German Perspective*, Hamburg: Institut für Finanzdienstleistungen.
18 For an extended discussion about the meaning of Hegel see the chapter dedicated to him in Gilje, Nils and Skirbekk, Gunnar (2001), *A History of Western Thought: From Ancient Greece to the Twentieth Century*, UK: Routledge; also Ziętek, Magdalena and Kaliniecki, Pawel, GK Chesterton and the Challenge of Poland, *The Distributist Review*, July 14, 2013. Available at http://distributistreview.com/mag/2013/07/g-k-chesterton-and-the-challenge-of-poland/.
19 See, for example, Wright, Erik Olin (2010), *Envisioning Real Utopias*, UK: Verso.
20 Collinson, Patrick and Jones, Rupert, Can I buy debt like the Occupy Wall Street activists did?, *Guardian*, November 13, 2013. Available at http://www.theguardian.com/world/shortcuts/2013/nov/13/can-i-buy-debt-like-occupy-wall-street.
21 For more information on this see Ross, Andrew (2014*)*, *Creditocracy: And the Case for Debt Refusal*, New York: OR Books.
22 Using this word, it has been said previously, can have negative connotations. I use it only to avoid confusion. In general I take the same view as London Economics writers who prefer the term "debt adjustment" to "bankruptcy." See London Economics (2011), *Study on Means to Protect Consumers in Financial Difficulty: Personal Bankruptcy, Datio in Solutum of Mortgages, and Restrictions on Debt Collection Abusive Practices*, London: London Economics.
23 In any case, bankruptcy or debt cancellation should be an option up until a lender proves there was "bad faith" before the transaction was carried out, the right to these options should be primary.
24 Griffiths, Margaret (2008), The Sustainability of Consumer Credit Growth in Late Twentieth Century Australia, *Journal of Consumer Studies & Home Economics*, Vol. 24, No. 1.

Discussion Points 131

25 Centre for Social Justice (2013), *Maxed Out*, UK: The Centre for Social Justice.
26 Eurofound (2012), *Household Debt Advisory Services in the European Union*, Brussels: Eurofound.
27 United States Census Bureau (2013), *Household Debt in the U.S.: 2000 to 2011*, US: United States Census Bureau; and Borné, Rebecca and Smith, Peter (2013), *High-Cost Overdraft Practices*, in Center for Responsible Lending, "The State of Lending in America & Its Impact on U.S. Households," Durham: Center for Responsible Lending.
28 Wilson, Therese (2008), Responsible Lending or Restrictive Lending Practices? Balancing Concerns Regarding Over-Indebtedness with Addressing Financial Exclusion, In Kelly-Louw, Michelle, Nehf, James P., and Rott, Peter (eds), *The Future of Consumer Credit Regulation: Creative Approaches to Emerging Problems*, Hampshire: Ashgate.
29 Chin, Pearl (2004), *Payday Loans: The Case for Federal Legislation*, Illinois: University of Illinois Law Review.
30 Griffiths, Margaret (2008), The Sustainability of Consumer Credit Growth in Late Twentieth Century Australia, *Journal of Consumer Studies & Home Economics*, Vol. 24, No. 1.
31 Royston, Sam and Rodrigues, Laura (2013), *Nowhere to Turn? Changes to Emergency Support*, London: The Children's Society.
32 Trumbull, Gunnar (2012), Credit Access and Social Welfare the Rise of Consumer Lending in the United States and France, *Politics and Society*, Vol. 40, No. 1.
33 Howell, Nicola and Wilson, Therese, Access to Consumer Credit: the Problem of Financial Exclusion in Australia and the Current Regulatory Framework, *Macquarie Law Journal*, Vol. 5.
34 Rivlin, Gary (2011), *Broke USA*, US: HarperBusiness.
35 Private conversation with Gerard Brody.
36 Osborne, Hilary, Payday Loans Market Faces Competition, *Guardian*, June 27, 2013. Available at http://www.theguardian.com/money/2013/jun/27/payday-loans-competition-inquiry-oft.
37 Phillips, Ben (2013), *NATSEM Household Budget Report: Cost of Living and Standard of Living Indexes for Australia*, Canberra: University of Canberra.
38 Lawrence, Mathew and Cooke, Graeme (2014), *Jumping the Shark: Building Institutions to Spread Access to Affordable Credit*, London: ippr.
39 Center for Financial Services Innovation, CFSI Study Reveals 15 Million US Consumers of Small-Dollar Credit Products, *Center for Financial Services Innovation*, August 22, 2012. Available at CFSI Study Reveals 15 million US Consumers of Small-Dollar Credit Products. See more at: http://www.cfsinnovation.com/content/cfsi-study-reveals-15-million-us-consumers-small-dollar-credit-products#sthash.G3KG6WYu.dpuf.

40 Consumer Finance Protection Bureau, Director Richard Cordray Remarks at the Payday Field Hearing, *Consumer Finance Protection Bureau*, March 25, 2014. Available at http://www.consumerfinance.gov/newsroom/director-richard-cordray-remarks-at-the-payday-field-hearing/.
41 Office of Fair Trading (2013), *Payday Lending: Compliance Report Final Report*, UK: Office of Fair Trading.
42 Rivlin, Gary (2011), *Broke USA*, US: HarperBusiness.
43 Moore, Elaine, Payday Lenders: Key Aspects of FCA Proposals, *Financial Times*, October 3, 2013. Available at http://www.ft.com/cms/s/0/2a3c0572-2c20-11e3-acf4-00144feab7de.html?siteedition=uk#axzz33kw8gM65.
44 Citizens Advice, Payday Lenders Need to Deliver on Promise to Check Loans are Affordable, *Citizens Advice*, May 15, 2013. Available at http://www.citizensadvice.org.uk/_/press_office20130515.
45 Goldsmith, Zac (2010), *Payday Loans: Helping Hand or Quicksand: Examining the Growth of High-Cost Short-Term Lending in Australia, 2002–2010*, Melbourne: Consumer Action Law Centre.
46 Ellison, Anne and Forster, Robert (2008), *Payday in Australia: A Research Study of the Use and Impact of Payday Lending in the Domestic Australian Market*, UK: Policis.
47 Montezmolo, Susanna (2013), *Payday Lending Abuses and Predatory Practices*, US: Center for Responsible Lending.
48 The letter is available at http://www.responsiblelending.org/payday-lending/research-analysis/AFR-Signers-Payday-Letter-to-CFPB-3-28-14.pdf.
49 Pew: Payday Solutions.
50 CRL—State of Lending.
51 Zywicki, Todd. (2010), Consumer Use and Government Regulation of Title Pledge Lending, *George Mason Law & Economics*, Research Paper No. 10-12.
52 Citizens Advice, What are Logbook Loans, Available at http://www.citizensadvice.org.uk/index/campaigns/current_campaigns/logbook-loans.htm.

7
Conclusion and Recommendations

Abstract: *Finally I conclude and add recommendations that can have, to varying degrees, a real positive impact to the regulation of consumer credit in general, and high-cost credit more specifically. The recommendations are divided into industry-specific interventions, ranging from caps on the cost of credit, bans on rollovers, and offering longer term loans, to wider interventions such as an annual levy placed on the payday lending industry to pay for its own regulation, uniform laws on all consumer credit to ensure lenders cannot circumvent rules, a Community Reinvestment Act as well as banking ordnances, to the development of responsible credit.*

Keywords: community; credit; debt

Packman, Carl. *Payday Lending: Global Growth of the High-Cost Credit Market.* New York: Palgrave MacMillan, 2014. DOI: 10.1057/9781137361103.0010.

In looking at the evidence internationally, where it is available, there seem to be a number of consistent themes: payday lending as a formalized industry as well as other forms of high-cost credit have been allowed to grow strongly in a number of countries, not because of a lack of credit opportunities, but often in addition to them. If we look at the countries where payday lending has played a big part in such a relatively small space of time, such as the UK, the US, and Australia for example, then we see it emerge in a context where consumer credit is already very dominant. There is interplay between growing debt profiles and the need to take on very high risk, high-cost credit, in countries that have to varying degrees rolled back models of the universal or partial welfare state and sought to allow citizens to prosper through greater take-up of private debt. While the recession of 2007 onward may appear as the event that tipped personal debt profiles over the edge in many countries growing debt profiles, particularly of unsecured debt, started to take place before then.

There is a common theme around the debt profiles of countries that grew as a result of deregulation in the 1980s, again in varying degrees across Europe, North America, parts of Australasia, and beyond. In those countries highlighted in this study we find a commonality of what might be called the neoliberal experiment, one whose primary aim is to give primacy the consumer and roll back the state, while being responsible for rising personal debt. On a local level those debt levels can have a very serious effect: debt distress that increases the risk of default on other debts, on bankruptcy, and on mental health.[1] At the various times when there has been heightened consciousness about the effects of debt, such as studies into overindebtedness in the EU or financial inclusion in the UK (which through no fault of those studying it typically begin when there is a crisis), it has been found that various financial products, for instance revolving overdrafts, have not been best suited to assist in returning indebted households to better financial progress. In recent times, with the rise of the formalized high-cost credit industry, which is distinct from mainstream financial institutions (but to varying degrees either a part of them or a provision that anticipates a gap in the market left by mainstream financial institutions), there has been even less evidence that taking on high-cost credit serves as a means to put finances in order; quite the contrary in some cases.

To the final conclusion, due to some of the common ways in which the high-cost credit industry operates across countries where its presence is most apparent it is justified to use rather broad stroke conclusions about it. It must be stressed again that more specific research is needed in all countries where high-cost credit has a presence on the grounds that it can be financially very damaging for households if policymakers ignore the small gains of industries deemed predatory. But what has been found so far, from the commonalities of the industry and general remarks made primarily about the industry in countries with the largest presence, is:

- there is a very high cost associated with this form of credit sold most frequently to those with the least capacity to afford it;
- the most profitable customers are those who return;
- offering rollover loans, also, is a profitable source of revenue;
- limited credit checking and affordability assessments are a disincentive for lenders as it can prove an expensive and time-consuming task, and in any case reviewing affordability may prove a distraction if profit maximization involves targeting a potential return custom base;
- a lack of competition has, in the main, meant that neither price review nor practice review is an incentive. What is apparent is at some level it might be necessary to apply a code of conduct (see the case of the UK and the Consumer Finance Association or Canada and the Canadian Payday Loan Association) but questions are still frequently raised about whether those codes are being met.

The business model of payday lending within the high-cost credit industry has not been designed primarily to improve the financial situation or future financial capability of its borrowers, and in a high number of instances it has been shown to do the opposite, therefore the general perception of the industry being predatory appears correct, to varying degrees in different localities. There is of course a degree to which policy makers and mainstream financial institutions have a part to play in the rise of the high-cost credit industry, but this cannot be used to absolve the industry itself. As it has been commented on previously to carry out fair business practices and employ methods of responsible lending will be of considerable cost to the industry.[2] This is because in looking at the evidence it would appear that the industry has been operating to a very poor standard of ethics, much to the benefit of its very recent and rapid growth rates. Before the 1990s it didn't exist, now it plays an increasingly important and high-profile part of the consumer credit market in many different countries around the world.

Do not ignore the small gains: When talking about the decision by Newcastle United Football Club to allow the payday lender Wonga.com sponsor its football strip and stadium, the outspoken critic of payday lending Stella Creasy MP used the analogy of Jurassic Park to explain the small but dangerous consumer credit lenders: "In the scenes with the raptors, we see that they are learning, they are adapting, and the same is true with these firms." The high-cost credit industry has been the raptor in the economic crisis, with the issue often being neglected or written off as little compared to the practices of large banks. But critics might say that this absolves payday lenders of the bad practices that they have become known for over the years. In saying payday lending in the UK is worth only around 2 percent of the total consumer credit market neglects to mention that from 2004 to 2014 it has gone from being worth £100m to £2.8bn (which is a conservative estimate by the Office of Fair Trading). Similarly in 1998 Australia's first payday lender was set up, and by 2001 around 82 payday lending businesses were offering approximately 12,800 loans a month. Now the industry is worth $800m. Ignoring the small gains of the small-dollar loans industry can, if history is any judge, be at a cost later on.

Cost caps: Macaulay and Leff have made the point previously that government often cedes regulatory power to private enterprises by allowing businesses to define the terms of commerce in industries in which competitive forces do not constrain the terms. This is having a damaging effect on those underserved by mainstream finance or community-oriented alternative finance. The case has been made that price caps can do what the market often can't, which is bring pricing to a point where borrowers benefit, and the notion that caps have an inherently consequential effect on the volume of illegal loan sharks has been shown to be false or at the very least inconclusive. Therefore, a consumer-oriented position would naturally tend toward installing price caps across the industry.

A ban on all rollovers: Rollovers have been shown time over to be the incentive by which unscrupulous lenders seek out profitable customers, who so happen to be the least financially resilient. Rollovers are also a very clear indication that the borrower is suffering from the credit they have received, and while consumers have both rights and responsibility under most country's laws, so too do lenders who as it would seem very often pass over their responsibilities in the pursuit for greater profit. Therefore, a ban on rollovers would omit one of the most contentious parts of the high-cost credit industry.

Longer terms: Lending initiatives from nonprofits that have tried to out-compete high-cost creditors with products with similar to theirs, but with a social conscience, have often said that one of the appeals of their credit is the longer term. Progreso Financiero in the United States and the CUOK loan from the London Mutual Credit Union in the UK both have longer terms but serve a similar cohort. As more lenders consider installment loans as their next possibility community-oriented lenders should stay one step ahead by offering products with longer terms, that if following those same models can be financed at scale.

Rigorous credit checking—5 percent is too much: Given the assault that incomes have had for the working poor in the richest countries, where high-cost credit is a regular feature today, it is perhaps not surprising that survey and market data, analyzed by Pew, have shown that monthly loan payments exceeding 5 percent of a borrower's individual gross monthly income are unaffordable. While this not only makes the case for loan repayments to never be over a certain proportion of a borrower's monthly income, it will also require lenders to be more vigilant in their credit checking. As shown in earlier chapters the incentive to omit credit checking from the application process is (a) because it provides an expense for the lenders, and (b) assessing affordability would be contrary to the means by which many lenders make the most profit, by return custom. The expense of a credit check might not seem worth the time if nonaffordability is a win situation. This can be avoided. Many states in the United States are already using real-time database systems such as Veritec to identify situations where someone is taking out what may be considered a troubling amount of loans. Both consumer credit regulators in the UK and Australia as of 2013 are consulting on whether to introduce a real-time database system, too. Having a system that can track payday loan use and other forms of high-cost credit is one way to ensure lenders lend responsibly, and regulators regulate sufficiently.

An annual levy placed on the entire payday loans industry to pay for its own regulation: Given the attention that regulators worldwide have had to give the high-cost credit industry, a sensible way of maintaining that regulatory focus would be to place a year-by-year levy on the whole industry that pays for the regulator. While the industry would say that it unfairly punishes the responsible lenders, it must be argued that irresponsible lending has become almost inseparable with payday lending, something the entire industry must take responsibility for.

Uniformity of laws in consumer credit to ensure that lenders can't expect to do business as usual with modified terms: The same laws that cover payday lending and high-cost credit, to ensure they cannot carry out irresponsible lending practices and get away with it, should be equally applicable to all bank and nonbank lending to ensure against all predatory practices.

An extended Community Reinvestment Act (CRA): Where the CRA has been operable in the United States it has had many critics even from ardent supporters. This is due to issues around ineffective enforcement rather than the principle of the CRA itself. This principle should be a best practice among all nations, and apply to all consumer creditors including payday lenders, whose reinvestment should be put into community-oriented finance for low-income households. Identifying and punishing discriminatory practices in banking should be widespread. In addition to the CRA, policymakers should consider following where other cities have led in banking oversight. The 2002 responsible banking ordinance in Philadelphia, for example, which stipulates that "Each depository must provide the City with an annual statement of community reinvestment goals including the number of small business loans, home mortgages, home improvement loans, and community development investments to be made within low and moderate-income neighborhoods in the City of Philadelphia."[3]

Incentives for credit unions and cooperative banks (nonprofits): Incentives ought to be given to alternative finance lenders such as credit unions or cooperative banks who lend in local communities that have seen dramatic rises in the volume of payday loan storefronts. Leniency regarding their capital requirements, that can often mean the difference between a credit union able to lend and offer savings accounts to low-income neighborhoods or not, is also something policymakers should consider.

The right to credit: The European Coalition for Responsible Credit has stated its commitment to "productive" credit that leads neither to impoverishment nor to overindebtedness. Government policymakers should do all that they can to facilitate the development of product credit and savings products that citizens can rely on as a right. There is of course a cost argument here: the less a nation's citizens are in hock to predatory lenders, the more they can save to fend off further financial shocks, spend in the productive economy, not sweetening the balances of the high-cost credit industry, and the closer they will be to being debt-free.

Notes

1. See, for example, Fitch, Chris et al. (2011), The Relationship between Personal Debt and Mental Health: a Systematic Review, *Mental Health Review Journal*, Vol. 16, No. 4, pp. 153–166.
2. Flannery, Mark J. and Samolyk, Katherine (2005), Payday Lending: Do the Costs Justify the Price?, *FDIC Center for Financial Research Working Paper*, No. 2005/09; and the comments made by Stan Keyes in the North America chapter.
3. Similar is Cleveland's law, enacted in 1991, one of the earliest responsible banking ordinances. San Jose in 2010, Seattle in 2011, and Pittsburgh, New York City, Los Angeles, Portland, Kansas City in 2012.

Index

Advertising 9, 11, 23, 50, 74, 81, 82, 89, 93, 115
Affordability assessments 75, 87, 116, 127–128, 135
Agarwal, Sumit 103
Aldinger, William 16
Ali, Paul 83
American Indian population (US) 102
  Tribes 105–106
Anderson v H&R Block, Inc. 17
Annualised Percentage Rates (APR) 49, 57, 62, 104, 109, 115,
Archbishop of Canterbury 46, 49
Ariovich, Laura 6, 11
Associated Press
Association of British Credit Unions Limited (ABCUL) (UK) 47
Australia 3, 6, 18, 60, 64, 73–94, 115–116, 122–123, 124, 127, 134, 136, 137
  Australian Capital Territory 74
  New South Wales 74, 76, 124
  Northern Territory 74
  Queensland 74, 76, 80, 88, 124
  South Australia 74
  Tasmania 74
  Victoria 74, 80
  Western Australia 74
Australian Financial Institutions Commission (Australia) 91
Australian Financial Review (Australia) 87
Australian Labor party (Australia) 89, 90
Australian Prudential Regulatory Authority (Australia) 92
Australian Securities and Investments Commission (Australia) 75, 81, 82, 88, 93, 94, 116
Austria 60, 61, 67
Authority for the Financial Markets (Netherlands) 62, 63

Bailey, Jeff 16
Bankruptcy 24, 25, 79, 80, 108, 121, 122, 134
Banks 5, 6, 9,10, 11, 13, 17, 18, 19, 20, 21, 24, 25, 26, 40, 42, 43, 46, 50, 59, 65, 66, 67, 68, 79, 84, 89, 91, 92, 93, 100, 108, 109, 110, 116, 119, 121, 122, 123, 136, 138
  Australia and New Zealand Banking Group 79
  Bank of America 12, 22, 25
  Bank of Spain 62
  Beneficial Corporation 16
  Commonwealth Bank 79

Index

Bank of America – *continued*
   First National Bank of Chicago 24
   Harris Trust and Savings Bank 24
   Household Finance Corp. 16
   HSBC 17
   Hudson County National Bank 11
   JP Morgan 22
   Macquarie Bank 86
   National Australia Bank 79, 90
   Northern Trust Company 24
   Reserve Bank of Australia 79
   Wells Fargo 16, 22
   Westpac 79
Beddows, Sarah 61, 117
Belgium 56, 60, 61
"Big Bang" 40, 122
Bizley, M.T.L 39
Bolles, John Augustus 10
Bombay "Five-Sixers" (India) 115
Bos, Wouter 62
Bridges, Sarah 44
British Bankers Association (UK) 67
Brody, Gerard 76, 90
Building Societies 40, 79, 116
Bureau for Investigative Journalism (UK) 116
Business Review Weekly 81

Calder, Lendol 99
Campbell, James Keith 79
Canada 17, 18, 31, 61, 107–108, 135
   Newfoundland 107
   Quebec 107
Canadian Payday Loan Association (Canada) 108, 135
Cantona, Eric 66
Capital requirements (for financial institutions) 68, 92, 138
Capitalism 6, 11, 119–120
Caskey, John 29–30, 102
Catholicism 57
Cato Institute (US) 109
Center for Financial Services Innovation (US) 102, 125
Center for Responsible Lending (US) 101, 107, 109, 120, 127, 128

Chin, Pearl 116
China 22, 115
Christianity 28
Citizens Advice (UK) 46, 126, 127, 128
Clark, Cornelius 11
Clinton, Bill 25, 26
Collard, Sharon 46–47
Community Development Credit Unions (see Credit Unions)
Community Development Finance Institutions (CDFIs) 47
Community Financial Services Association of America, The (US) 2
Competition 60, 108, 116, 125, 126, 135
Competition Commission (UK) 125, 126
Conservative party (UK) 39, 46, 49
Consumer Action Law Centre (Australia) 42, 76–77, 85, 86, 90, 127
Consumer Federation of America (US) 27, 30
Consumer Finance Association (UK) 118, 119, 135
Consumer Finance Protection Bureau (US) 103, 104, 105, 124, 126, 128
Consumer Focus (UK) 20
Consumerism 3, 6,
Cordray, Richard 104–105
Creasy, Stella, MP 45–46, 136
Credit
   Auto title loans (See Car title loans)
   Car title loans 101, 104, 128
   Cash checking 2, 37
   Doorstep credit 43, 56
   Flitskrediet ("flash credit") 62
   Installment lending 6–8, 13, 16, 78, 107, 128, 137
   Overdrafts 42, 43, 116, 134
   Pawnbroking 2, 5, 21, 22, 30, 37, 38–39, 43
   Payday lending 2, 3, 4, 16–31, 37, 43–50, 60–66, 74–90, 102–111, 115–128, 134–138
   Salary lending 2, 14, 15, 22, 115, 117

Index

Credit Cards
  American Express 12
  Barclaycard 40
  Carte Blanche credit card 12
  Mastercard 12, 29
  Visa 12, 29
Credit Research Center, The (UK) 102
Credit Union Expansion Project (UK) 47, 48
Credit Unions 9, 11, 46, 47, 48, 50, 66, 67, 68, 79, 89, 91–93, 108–110, 120, 137, 138
  CaissesPopulaires Desjardins (now Desjardins Group) (US) 109
  Fitzroy and Carlton Community Credit Union (Australia) 91
  London Mutual Credit Union (UK) 48, 137
  Schulze-Delitzsch Credit Cooperatives (Germany) 66
Crowther Committee (UK) 39
Cummins, Peter 86
CUOK (See London Mutual Credit Union)
Curruthers, Bruce G. 5
Cyrus McCormack 6
Czech Republic 61, 62

Debt 2–3, 6, 9, 11, 12, 13, 43–45, 58–60, 83–87, 99–102, 122–123, 134
  Debt collection 15, 126
  Debt distress 3, 121, 134
  Household debt 65, 83, 100, 123
Delaney, Janet 19
Deloitte 116
Demos (UK) 44–45
Denmark 61
Department for Business, Industry and Skills (UK) 49
Department for Trade and Industry (UK) 39, 41, 124
Department for Work and Pensions (UK) 47
Deregulation 17, 40, 64, 79, 99, 100, 122–123, 134
Desjardins, Alphonse 109

DeStefano, Sam 15
Disney, Richard 44
Drummond, Matthew 87

Ellison, Anna 45
Ernst & Young 117
Estonia 61, 67
Eubank, Earle 13
European Coalition for Responsible Banking (EU) 59, 138
European Commission 42, 56, 57, 58, 63–64, 67
European Economic Community 56
European Union 56–57, 59, 60, 64, 66–67

Facebook 62
Family Resources Survey (UK) 42
Federal Court (Australia) 81
Federal Deposit Insurance Corporation (US) 102, 110
Federal Reserve Board (US) 26, 100, 101
Federal Trade Commission (US) 23, 104, 105
FICO (US) 103
Filene, Edward 9
Financial Conduct Authority (UK) 49, 126
Financial crisis of 2007–2012 40, 57, 120, 122
Financial Inclusion 40–43, 50, 51, 59, 78, 91, 134
Financial Inclusion Centre (UK) 43
Financial Inclusion Taskforce (UK) 41–42
Financial Institutions Scheme (Australia) 91–92
Financial Services and Superannuation (Australia) 74
Financial Services Users Group (EU) 67
Financial Times 37
Financialization 57, 60, 64, 100, 120
Finland 61, 67
Fishbein, Allan. J 25

Five for six (see salary lending) 14
Flannery, Mark, J. 19, 84
Founding Fathers, the 10
France 41, 56, 60, 61, 63, 65, 67, 119, 123

Generation Debt 58
Germany 41, 56, 60, 61, 63, 66, 67, 119,
Gibbons, Damon 39
Gilliam, Zac 86
Goldsmith, Raymond 99
Graeber, David 28
Graves, Steven 27
Great Depression 5, 12
Griffiths, Margaret 79, 122
Groff, Nathan 106
Guttman, Robert 99

Heath, Edward 39
Hegel, G.W.F. 119–120
Higgins, Jim 27
Hilton, William Barron 12
Hispanic population (US) 102, 110
Holland (See Netherlands)
House of Lords (UK) 49
House of Representatives (Australia) 77
House of Representatives (US) 28
Household income 9, 13, 16, 18, 19, 31, 41, 44, 58, 64, 65, 66, 78–79, 83–84, 88, 101, 103, 107, 109, 119, 122, 123, 138
Howell, Nicola 91–92
Huls, Nick, J.H. 58
Hungary 61
Hyman, Louis 7, 11

Illegal Loan Sharks 5, 16, 118–119, 124, 136
  UK 40, 41, 45, 49
  Netherlands 61
Infosys Technologies Ltd 81
Institute for Public Policy Research (UK) 125
Interest rates 2, 10, 11, 17, 23, 39–40, 41, 45, 48–49, 61–65, 74–75, 77, 79, 80, 82, 89, 90, 93, 99–100, 104, 105, 122–125

Ireland 40, 60–61, 67
Italy 56, 61

Johns, Phil 88, 90, 93
Johnson, Robert 22
Jones, Allan 19, 21
Joseph Rowntree Foundation (UK) 44
Jurassic Park 136

Keyes, Stan 108
Koning, Martin 100

Labour Party (UK) 37
Latvia 61, 67
Lazzarato, Maurizo 64, 65
Leff, Art 136
Legal Aid Society 7
Leyton, Andrew 46
Liberal Democrat party (UK) 46
Liberal Party (Canada) 108
Lithuania 67
Living Wage (UK) 44
Lowden, Frank 15
Low income (See Working poor)
Luxembourg 56

Macaulay, Stewart 136
Macedonia 67
Mackay, Frank. J 16
Macy's 8, 9
Malta 61
Mann, Ronald 103
Marquette National Bank of Minneapolis vs. First of Omaha Service Corp. 17
Marsico, Richard 25–26
Martin, Nathalie 103
Mathews, Race 91
Matz, Debbie 109
Mayer, Robert 13–14, 22
McAteer, Mick 61, 117
McNess, Elizabeth 76
Melbourne Law School 83
Melzer, Brian 103, 125
Mexico 18, 62, 110–111

144 *Index*

Microfinance
  Fair Loans Foundation
    (Australia) 93
  Good Money Hub (Australia) 92
  Good Shepherd Youth & Family
    Service (Australia) 90
  No Interest Loans Scheme
    (Australia) 90
  The Brotherhood St Laurence
    (Australia) 90
Middle Class 2, 9, 14, 16
Miliband, David 37
Moldova 67
MoneySmart (Australia) 82
Montgomerie, Johnna 100
Move Your Money campaign (UK) 66
Movement for Change (UK) 37

National Consumer Law Center 109
National Credit Union Administration
  (US) 109
National Financial Services Federation
  (Australia) 88
National Health Service (UK) 110
Neoliberalism 58, 60, 64, 100, 120
Netherlands 56, 60, 61, 62, 67, 124
New York City Provident Loan Society
  (US) 5, 9
New Zealand 6, 79
Newcastle United Football Club 136
Norway 60

Occupy Wall Street 120–121
Office for Budget Responsibility
  (UK) 43
Office of Fair Trading (UK) 45, 117,
  124, 126, 136
Operation Chokepoint (US) 109
Osborne, George 49, 74
Overindebtedness 56, 57, 58, 60, 61, 65,
  99, 121, 122, 134, 138

Palmerston, Lord 38
Payday lenders
  ACE Cash Express (US) 22, 31, 101,
    108

Advance America (US) 21, 22, 101
Australian Money Exchange
  (Australia) 80, 123
Betaaldag.nl (Netherlands) 63
Big State Pawn (US) 18
Cash America (US) 2, 18, 22, 31, 101
Cash America Mexico (Mexico) 18
Cash and Cheque Express (UK) 101
Cash Bob (Netherlands) 63
Cash Converters (Australia) 42, 80,
  82, 83, 85, 86–90, 93, 123, 127,
Cash Store (Australia) 81, 83
CashNetUSA (US) 18
Check Into Cash (US) 19, 21, 101
Cheque Exchange (Australia) 80,
  123
CNG Financial (US) 101
Credito Pocket (Spain) 62
DFC Global (US) 37, 101, 108
DollarsDirect Australia
  (Australia) 18
DollarsDirect Canada (Canada) 18
EZ Money (US) 101
First Cash Financial Services
  (US) 101
Kreditech (Germany) 62, 66
LendUp (US) 110
Loan Mart (US) 31
Money Mart (Canada) 31
Money Mart (US) 101, 108
Mr Money (US) 22
Nimble Australia (Australia) 82–83
Progreso (US) 110, 137
QC Holdings (US) 101
QuickQuid (UK) 18
Speedy Cash (UK) 37
The Money Shop (UK) 31, 37
Wonga.com (UK) 46, 49, 62–63,
  66, 136
Zippy Cash (Canada) 108
Peterson, Christopher 24, 26, 27–28
Pew Charitable Trusts (US) 31
Pew Research Center (US) 103, 105,
  107, 128, 137
Pletz, John 30
Plihon, Dominique 99

Poland 61, 62, 63, 67
Policis 41–42, 84–86, 119, 127
Portas, Mary 116
Portugal 61
Poverty 13, 22, 26, 44, 57, 83, 86, 120, 125,
  Working poor 2, 14, 16, 18, 20–22,
    27, 44, 64, 92, 115, 137
Price caps 42, 119, 136
Protestantism 57

Ramsay, Iains 107
Regulation
  Act on Financial Supervision
    (Netherlands) 63
  Banking Reform Bill (UK) 49
  Bankruptcy Act of 1898 (US) 24
  Bills of Sales Act (Australia) 78
  Community Reinvestment Act
    of 1977 (US) 5, 19, 24, 67, 104,
    109, 138
  Consumer Credit (Regulation and
    Advice) Bill 2010–2012 (UK) 45
  Consumer Credit Act of 1974
    (UK) 39, 115
  Consumer Credit and Corporations
    Amendment (Enhancements) Bill
    of 2011 (Cth) (Australia) 74
  Consumer Credit Directive of 2008
    (EU) 57, 59, 63, 65, 124
  Consumer Credit Legislation
    Amendment (Enhancements) Act
    of 2012 (Australia) 74
  Credit Act of 1984 (Australia) 79
  Credit Union Act of 1979 (UK) 48
  Criminal Code Act (Canada) 108
  Depository Institutions Deregulation
    and Monetary Control Act 1980
    (US) 17, 123
  Disclosure Directive (EU) 67
  Distance Selling Directive for
    Financial Services of 2002 (EU) 56
  Dodd–Frank Wall Street Reform
    and Consumer Protection Act
    (US) 104
  Equal Credit Opportunity Act
    of 1974 (US) 24

  Fair Housing Act of 1968 (US) 24
  Financial Corporations Act of 1974
    (Australia) 79
  Financial Services Act of 2012
    (UK) 49
  Hire Purchase Acts (Australia) 78
  Home Mortgage Disclosure Act
    of 1975 (US) 24, 25
  Loan Shark Act (US) (See Uniform
    Small Loan Law)
  Military Lending Act of 2007
    (US) 104
  Moneylenders Act of 1900 (UK) 38
  Moneylenders Act of 1927 (UK) 39,
    80
  National Bank Act (US) 17
  National Consumer Credit
    Protection Act 2009 (Cth)
    (Australia) 74, 75, 81
  Pawnbroking Act of 1872 (UK) 38
  Sale of Goods Act (Australia) 78
  Second Banking Directive of 1989
    (US) 99
  Truth in Lending Act (US) 23–24,
    26, 104, 115,
  Uniform Small Loan Law (US) 9, 15,
    17, 22, 23, 105, 106
Reifner, Udo 41, 56, 59, 62–64, 113
Resolution Foundation, The (UK) 44
Responsible Banking Ordinances
  (US) 138
Rivlin, Gary 16, 18, 19, 20, 21, 22, 27,
  105, 124, 126
Rollover loans 20, 105, 106, 107, 108,
  126–127, 135, 136
Romania 61, 67, 68
Rowlingson, Karen 46
Royal Melbourne Institute of
  Technology 85
Russell Sage Foundation (US) 9, 23
Russia 62, 67
Ryder, Dudley 38

Samolyk, Katherine 19, 84
Savings Gateway (UK) 42
Scheim, David. E 15

Scott, John 38
Searle, Jane 81
Sears, Roebuck & Company 8
Sharkey, John, Lord 49
Shorten, Bill 74, 89
Shulze-Delitzsch, Hermann 66
Skiba, Paige Marta 103, 117
Slovenia 61
Small-Dollar Loan Pilot Programme (See Pew Research Center)
SMS payday lending 66, 68, 124
Social Fund (UK) 46–47
Socialist Party (Netherlands) 62
Sopranos, The 13
South America 110
Spain 61, 62, 66, 67
Spector, Mary 31
St Basil 28
Stango, Victor 109
StepChange (UK) 44
Sutcliffe, Gerry 41
Sweden 61
Symon, Mike 90

T.C. Power and Bro. (US) 8
Teletrack (US) 103
Thatcher, Margaret 40
The Resolution Foundation (UK) 44
Thrift, Nigel 46
Tobacman, Jeremy 103, 117
Trumbull, Gunnar 65
Tweedie, Stephen 29

UK Treasury (UK) 41
Ukraine 67
Underconsumptionist theory 12
United Kingdom
  Barking 37
  Chelsea 37
  Ilford 37
  Kilburn 37
  Richmond 37
  Wood Green 37
  Westminster 37
United States
  California 106–107, 109

Colorado 21, 107, 118–119
District of Columbia 106
Florida 29, 31, 49, 106
Illinois 15, 106, 128
Indiana 106
Louisiana 31
Michigan 106
Missouri 31
New Mexico 106, 128
North Dakota 106
Oklahoma 106
Oregon 21, 31
Pennsylvania 108
Philadelphia 138
South Carolina 28, 29, 106
Texas 9, 18, 29, 31, 108
Virginia 21, 29, 106
Washington 31, 106
University of Bristol 42
  Personal Finance Research Centre 42, 47, 49
University of California 109
University of Queensland 85
US Postal Service Inspector General (US) 110
US Public Interest Research Group (US) 27, 30
Usury 7, 9, 10, 17, 18, 27, 28, 56–57, 59, 61, 62, 64, 107, 120, 123, 124, 125

Veritec 93, 106, 137

Wall Street Journal 16
Wallis Inquiry Reforms (Australia) 92
Wal-Mart 20
Wassam, Clarence 14, 117
Webster, Billy 21
Welfare 11, 12, 14, 64, 65, 85, 121, 123, 134
  Centrelink (Australia) 82, 85, 91, 92
  Scandinavian welfare model 65
  Revenu de solidarité active (France) 64
Whyte, William, H. 99
Wilson, Therese 91, 92
Working Class 5, 11, 37
Working poor 2, 14, 16, 18, 20, 115, 137

CPSIA information can be obtained at www.ICGtesting.com
Printed in the USA
BVOW05*1404240914

367982BV00001B/1/P